System Administration for Oracle

E-Business Suite

Personal Edition

SYSADMIN_P2007V3.1

System Administration for Oracle E-Business Suite
by ir. Roel A. Hogendoorn MSc

Illustrations by Gulzar Junaid

Any trademarked names are acknowledged only upon the first appearance
within this document and are used explicitly for editorial purposes.

The author and publisher have taken due care in preparation of this book, but
make no expressed or implied warranty of any kind and assume no
responsibility for errors or omissions. Therefore, the author and publisher
shall be held harmless from any liability subsequent or consequent to the
content of this document.

ISBN: 978-1-4357-0075-8

Table of Contents

Introduction

Oracle ® E-Business Suite R11i, also known as Oracle Applications, is a large and rather complex suite of interacting products. The documentation provided with it, in the form of Installation Guides, User Guides and Technical Reference Manuals, is so huge in size that it doesn't even fit on a cd and might therefore discourage any learning attempt.

This book aims to help you finding your way around this product suite and make your learning process quicker and more efficient by introducing you to the most important functions you will come across in your job as System Administrator. We hope that in this way you will become more aware of your role within your organization and most important, that you will also be able to enjoy learning and working with Oracle.

Each chapter of this book will cover the key functions and will be structured as follows:

- *description of the main features and components*
- *practical guided exercises with explanations and with related screen shots*
- *challenging exercises to get more familiar with each function*
- *a brief summary of the chapter content*

Chapter 1

Function Security

One of the main tasks of a System Administrator is to control user access to the system. The Oracle E-Business Suite, as every modern system, works with a username / password combination to login. Function security allows you to define users, and grant them privileges in relation to screens, reports and request sets.

This chapter will introduce you first to the main components of the Function Security. Then we will have a look at some examples on how to create a user, and grant, restrict or extend user privileges. At the end of the chapter, you will be able to practice all this with some exercises on Function Security.

1.1. What is Function Security?

Function security allows you to define users, and grant them privileges in relation to screens, reports and request sets. Function Security is based on Responsibilities.

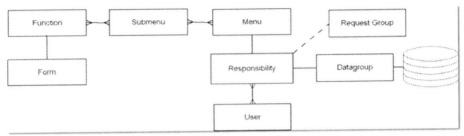

Illustration 1.1: The Function Security-schema

- A responsibility is a role or a job function. Oracle E-Business Suite includes predefined responsibilities such as 'System Administrator'. A user can be assigned to multiple responsibilities.
- A user is how you log-on.
- To each responsibility corresponds one menu, called Navigator menu which appears when you click on a responsibility.
- This navigator menu consists of several levels of submenus, which lead up to functions.
- Each function is linked to a Form, and can include parameters.
- Each Form is linked to an existing Form (*.fmx*).
- A responsibility can have a Request Group. A Request Group contains Concurrent Programs and Sets which can be run within a responsibility.
- The Datagroup is a list of Applications with database user names and passwords. It establishes the connection to the database.

User

A user owns a login user name and a password to enter the system.

Illustration 1.2: Login screen

The username / password combination is not case sensitive. In some companies you might be required to use the employee number as username, therefore the login username might look like 1289.217.364. This can be very useful in large organizations. However, you should be aware that there is a difference between a user and a HR Person as explained below.

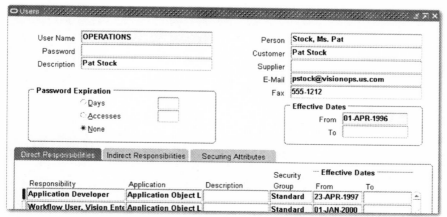

Illustration 1.3: System Administrator > Security > User > Define

HR Person

An HR person is an entity created in HR referring to a real person such as for example, 'John Smith' and all his personal data (date of birth, social security number, email address etc). A person can be linked to a user. Please be careful not to link the same person to two users, since this may cause problems within the approval Workflows.

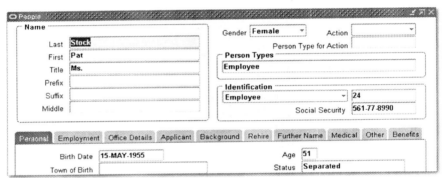

Illustration 1.4: Human Resources, Vision Enterprises > People > Enter and Maintain

Responsibility

A responsibility is a role or a job function. A user who is logged in, works within the scope of the responsibilities assigned to him/her. Normally, users have multiple responsibilities and they can switch between responsibilities using the 'hat-icon', or via File > Switch Responsibility. Also Multi-org characteristics depend on user responsibilities. In our example, John Smith who works for 'General Ledger, Germany', will have access to German data.

Illustration 1.5: Switch Responsibility

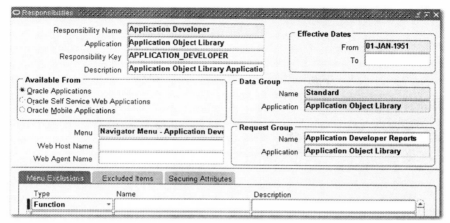

Illustration 1.6: System Administrator> Security > Responsibility > Define

Menu

Menus are displayed in the main Navigator screen. In the Menus screen you are able to assign privileges to access functions and

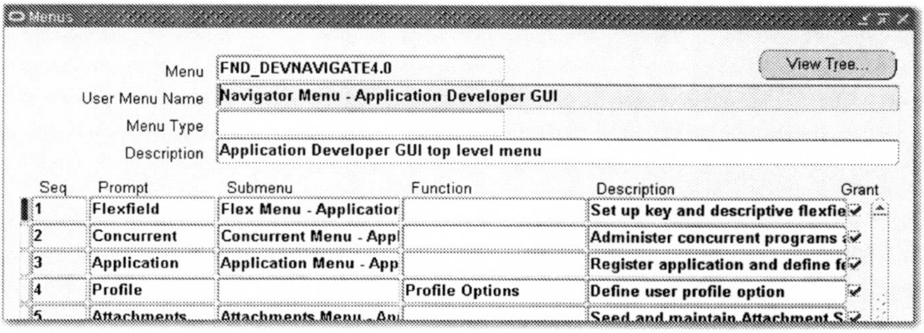

Illustration 1.7: System Administrator > Application > Menu

submenus through a menu and even the Process-tab page can be assigned to it.

Note: always search on the field "User Menu Name"

Function

A function executes a Form (screen). A function can use parameters (as defined in the Form). The same form can appear twice in a menu, but with different parameters. A standard parameter is QUERY_ONLY=YES.

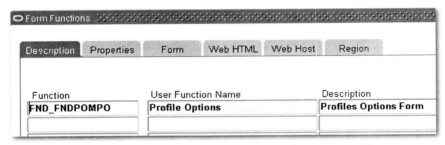

Illustration 1.8: System Administrator > Application > Function

Note: always search on the field "User Function Name"

Subfunction

A subfunction is a function which is not visible in the menu. This can be achieved in two ways:
1. by not giving it a prompt, and making it of the type 'function'
2. by giving it a prompt, and making it of the type 'subfunction'

A subfunction should be used to enable the end-user to open a form, but not directly from the menu. Example: you have a screen with some items and a screen which indicates the number of items in stock. This second screen can be opened through a button on the first screen. The user must have access to the second screen, otherwise an error message will appear. However, the user is not supposed to open the screen directly. In such a case you can use a subfunction.

Form

A Form indicates to eBS where the actual compiled Developer form (the *.fmx*) is located. To do this it uses a base path (the main directory) of an Application. Example: if in the Form is indicated that the *.fmx* can be found in General Ledger, the actual fmx will be located in $GL_TOP/forms/US on the Application Server.

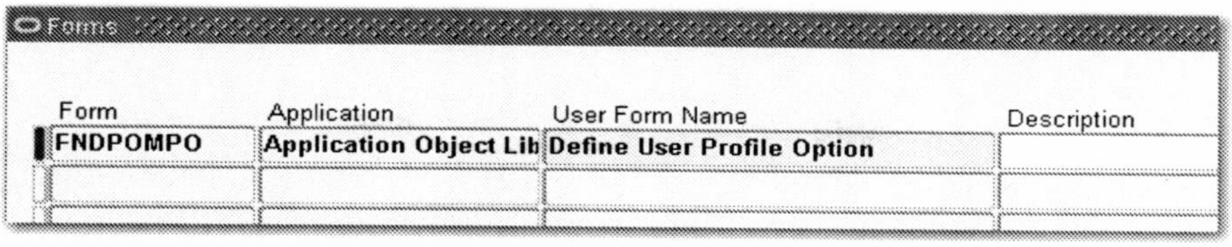

Form	Application	User Form Name	Description
FNDPOMPO	Application Object Lib	Define User Profile Option	

Illustration 1.9: Application Developer > Application > Form

Tip: search on the field "User Form Name" with the value found in the Function screen on the Form tab.

Data Group

The Data Group establishes the connection to the database. You will probably never work in the datagroup since this is normally a task of the Applications Database Administrator.

For changing the passwords on DB and eBS-level, you can use the tool FNDCPASS.

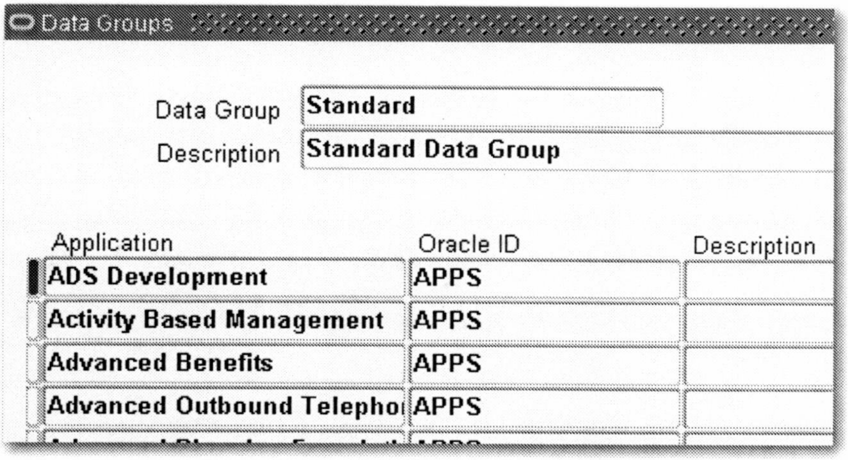

Data Group   **Standard**

Description   **Standard Data Group**

Application	Oracle ID	Description
ADS Development	APPS	
Activity Based Management	APPS	
Advanced Benefits	APPS	
Advanced Outbound Telepho|	APPS	

Illustration 1.10: System Administrator > Security > Oracle > Data Group

Concurrent Program

A Current Program is normally a report, purge script or similar that runs in the background, and that can be scheduled. Concurrent Programs, i.e. programs that can run in parallel, contain parameters which are passed to the program. Concurrent Programs will be discussed in more detail in chapter 4 on starting on page 59.

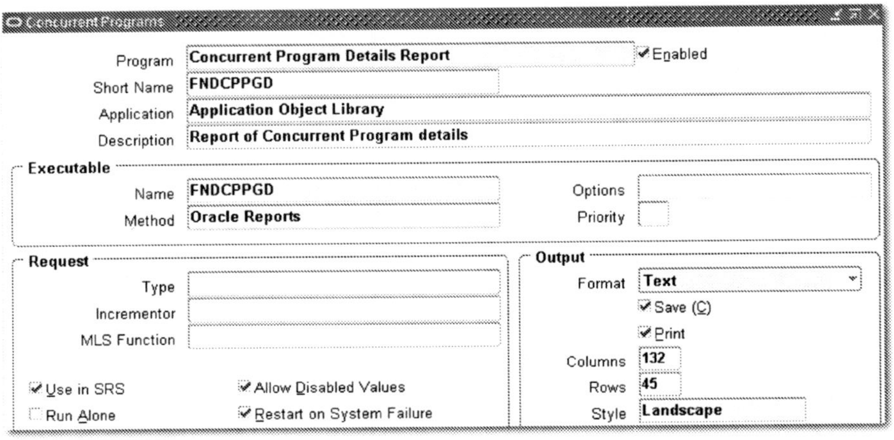

Illustration 1.11: System Administrator > Concurrent > Program > Define

Request Set

A Request Set is a set of Concurrent Programs which can be requested together, and whose parameters can be shared and passed.

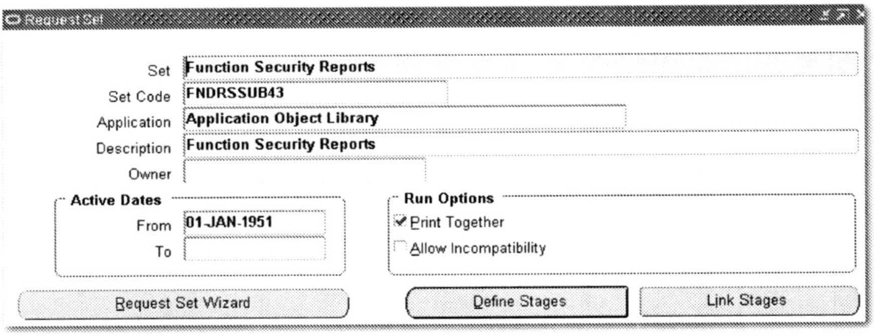

Illustration 1.12: System Administrator > Requests > Set

Request Group

A Request Group contains the Concurrent Programs, and Request Sets that a responsibility can execute.

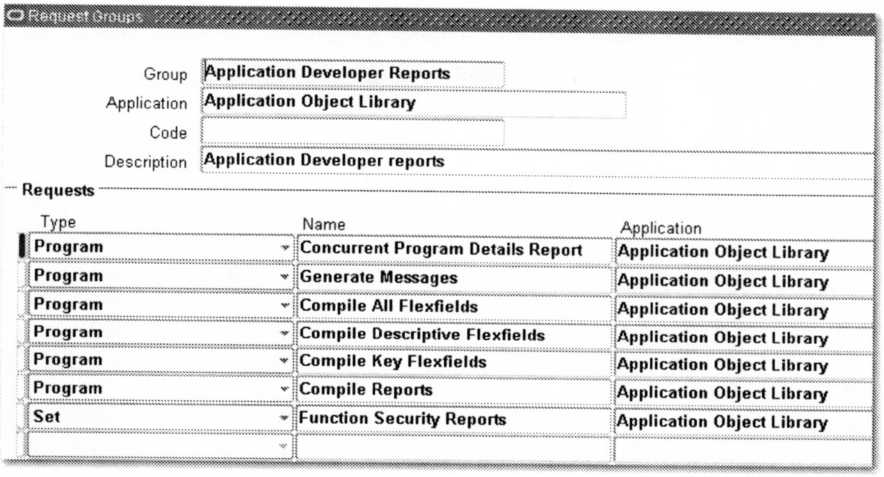

Type	Name	Application
Group	Application Developer Reports	
Application	Application Object Library	
Code		
Description	Application Developer reports	

Requests

Type	Name	Application
Program	Concurrent Program Details Report	Application Object Library
Program	Generate Messages	Application Object Library
Program	Compile All Flexfields	Application Object Library
Program	Compile Descriptive Flexfields	Application Object Library
Program	Compile Key Flexfields	Application Object Library
Program	Compile Reports	Application Object Library
Set	Function Security Reports	Application Object Library

Illustration 1.13: System Administrator > Security > Responsibility > Request

Application

Functionally: a group of forms, reports, scripts and tables with a common purpose. Technically: a directory on the application server (the base path, to separate the forms and reports from other applications) and a schema in the database (to separate the data).

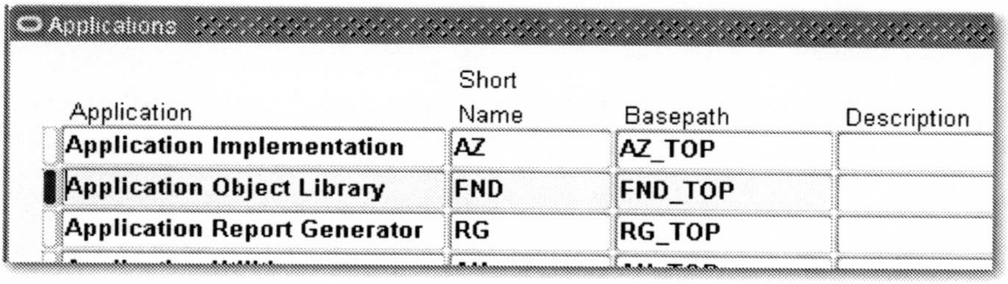

Application	Short Name	Basepath	Description
Application Implementation	AZ	AZ_TOP	
Application Object Library	FND	FND_TOP	
Application Report Generator	RG	RG_TOP	

Illustration 1.14: System Administrator > Application > Register

1.2. Guided exercises

Create a user

Tip: Before you start, always make notes of what you are going to do.

Create User PRACT01, with the following Responsibilities: General Ledger, Vision Operations (USA) and Inventory, Vision Operations (USA). The user must be active for this week only.

Step 1: Login with username / password: operations / welcome.

Step 2: Go to the Navigator column on the left side, where the Responsibilities are displayed, and click on the responsibility "System Administrator".

Step 3: Go to the right column where the Forms are displayed, and click the Form: Security: User > Define

Step 4: The Form opens automatically in the Maintenance mode (yellow and white fields). A new user can be created directly. Enter the User Name: PRACT01, and enter the remaining required fields:

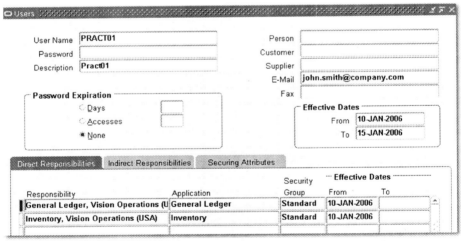

(The field email is important when Oracle Alert is used in the company).

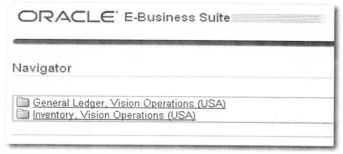

Step 5: Save, logout, and login as the new user. Change the password to oracle.

Create a user with restricted access privileges

Create a user (Pract01lim) who can access the General Ledger, Vision Operations (USA) responsibility, but has no privileges for the Setup possibilities.

Tip: since rights always relate to responsibilities, and not directly to users, a new responsibility must be created.

Step 1: Create user Pract01lim, with no responsibilities for the moment.

Step 2: Search for the General Ledger, Vision Operations (USA) responsibility:

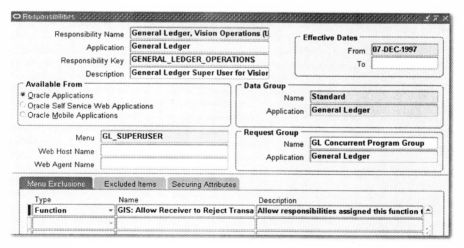

Step 3: Create a new responsibility in the same way, and give it the name XXORG General Ledger, Visions Operations (USA) limited. Then, exclude the submenu that you do not need.

Tip: If you are not so sure about which menu you should exclude, go to Application > Menu, search for the Menu GL_SUPERUSER and click "View Tree", this will provide you with much more information.

Responsibility Name	XXORG General Ledger, Vision Oper:
Application	General Ledger
Responsibility Key	XXORG_GENERAL_LEDGER_OPRATIC
Description	Adapted: without Setup

Effective Dates

From	10-JAN-2006
To	

Available From
- ⦿ Oracle Applications
- ○ Oracle Self Service Web Applications
- ○ Oracle Mobile Applications

Data Group

Name	Standard
Application	General Ledger

Menu	GL_SUPERUSER
Web Host Name	
Web Agent Name	

Request Group

Name	GL Concurrent Program Group
Application	General Ledger

Menu Exclusions | Excluded Items | Securing Attributes

Type	Name	Description
Function	GIS: Allow Receiver to Reject Transa	Allow responsibilities assigned this function t
Menu	GL_SU_SETUP	

Step 4: Link this responsibility to Pract01lim, logout and login as Pract01lim.

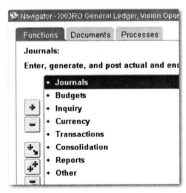

24

Grant and restrict report privileges

Grant to user Pract01lim report privileges for reports "Active Users" and "Active Responsibilities". The other reports privileges currently granted to this user must be removed.

Step 1: Create a new Request Group, with the two reports in it.

Group	XXORG_GL_LIMITED	
Application	General Ledger	
Code		
Description	RequestGroup with only two reports	

Requests

Type	Name	Application
Program	Active Users	Application Object Libr
Program	Active Responsibilities	Application Object Libr

Step 2: Link this Request Group to the responsibility defined in the previous example:

Responsibility Name	XXORG General Ledger, Vision Oper:
Application	General Ledger
Responsibility Key	XXORG_GENERAL_LEDGER_OPRATI(
Description	Adapted: without Setup

Effective Dates

From	10-JAN-2006
To	

Available From
- ⦿ Oracle Applications
- ○ Oracle Self Service Web Applications
- ○ Oracle Mobile Applications

Data Group

Name	Standard
Application	General Ledger

Menu	GL_SUPERUSER
Web Host Name	
Web Agent Name	

Request Group

Name	XXORG_GL_LIMITED
Application	General Ledger

Step 3: Logout, and login as Pract01lim. Test if it works in Other : Report > Run.

Create a custom menu

Grant user Pract01lim access privileges to the screens "Monitor Users" and "Network Test". As you know, screens (Forms) are linked to Functions, which are linked to Menus which are linked to Responsibilities (see page 14). Since screens cannot be linked directly to a user, you will need to create a custom menu.

Step 1: Find out how the function names that you are looking for. How? Refer to the tip on page 24, and be aware that the two screens you are going to add are also to be found in the System Administrator responsibility.

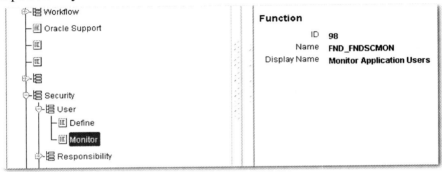

Ok, now you know the names of the functions: "Monitor Application Users" and "Network Test".

Step 2: Now create a menu with two entries: the two functions as shown below.

Seq	Prompt	Submenu	Function	D
10	Monitor Users		Monitor Application Use	
20	Network Test		Network Test	

Menu: XXORG_SYSADMIN_SMALL
User Menu Name: XXORG_SYSADMIN_SMALL
Menu Type:
Description:

Step 3: Create a new Responsibility and include the custom menu in it.

Step 4: Add the responsibility to user Pract01lim. Logout and login as Pract01lim.

Create a query-only form

Grant user Pract01lim privileges to use the screen "View Responsibilities". This screen should be Query-only, and you need to add it to the custom menu created in the previous Guided Exercise.

Step 1: Find the base function. Since you need to create a Function with a parameter, first find the name of the function pointing to the Responsibilities Screen. The best way to do this is querying the System Administrator menu called "Navigator Menu - System Administrator GUI". Query this menu and click on "View Tree": The name of the function is "Responsibilities".

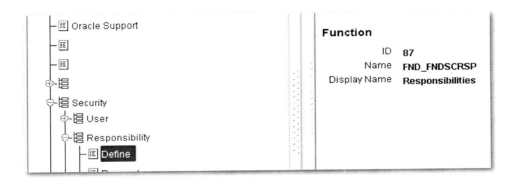

Step 2: Add the copied and modified base function.

Remember to fill in all the required fields, as you have done for the Responsibilities entry, and fill in the Parameters field:

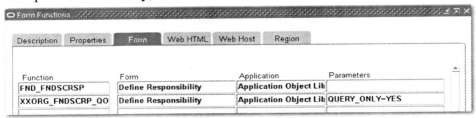

Step 3: Add the function to the menu defined in the previous Guided Exercise, logout and login as Pract01lim to test it.

1.3. Exercises

Naming standards in the exercises

- all components that you are going to create should start with XX<ORG>##, where <ORG> stands for a three letter abbreviation of your organization,
- and ## stands for your initials
- For example if you work for Nike and your name is John Smith, an eBS username should look like this: XXNKEJS_user_lim.

1. Create a user with the following responsibilities: Assets, Vision Operations (USA) and Cash Management, Vision Operations (USA).
2. Create a user with restricted privileges, who has access to Assets, Vision Operations (USA), but no privileges for the menu Mass Additions.
3. This restricted user should be able to run only the reports "Additions by Source Report" and "Reserve Detail Report".
4. Grant the restricted user the privileges for the screens "Monitor Users" and "Network Test".
5. Grant the restricted user the privileges for the screen "View Users". This screen must be Query-only.

1.4. Summary

This chapter introduced you to the use of Responsibilities, Menus, Functions and Request Groups in controlling user access rights. It gave you some explanations on how existing responsibilities and functions can be modified through menu exclusions and function parameters. We had a closer look at some examples on how to create a user and grant him privileges. This chapter ends with some useful exercises on the Function Security.

Chapter 2

Role Based Access Control

The Role Based Access Control is an extension of the Function Security. In this chapter, you'll first learn why this can be useful and what can be dangerous to use. Then, you'll be introduced to the characteristics of a Role and you will learn how to work with Delegated Administration and Data Security. Finally, you will be able to practice all this with some exercises concerning RBAC.

2.1. What is Role Based Access Control?

Before 11.5.10 the only method for granting rights to users was through the use of responsibilities. This gives the following problems:
- difficult to maintain
  - who is assigned to which responsibilities?
  - how can I easily revoke rights from my Inventory users?
- easy to make mistakes

Therefore, in the new release 11.5.10 Oracle has added the RBAC , Role Based Access Control, to its security model.
Initially, a Role contains one or more responsibilities.

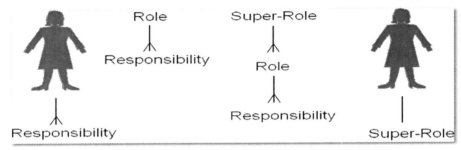

Illustration 2.1: Roles containing several Responsibilities.

The new security model does not replace the previous model based on responsibilities, but is built on top of it. For this purpose a new responsibility was created: User Management. This new responsibility allows to create, add or remove user roles.

Warning: RBAC is new and quite unstable

RBAC is new in eBS 11.5.10, and unfortunately not always as stable as you might expect. More stability and usability is offered by the possibility to link responsibilities to roles. Nonetheless, special role characteristics seem to be less stable. It is advisable to begin your work with responsibilities linked to roles, and eventually expand it to the role characteristics if needed.

2.2. Role characteristics

- Permission: rights in OA_FRAMEWORK-pages
- User Administration: possibility to reset password etc.
- Organization Administration: do above action on Partner Organizations
- Role Administration: the user becomes sub-administrator for certain roles (in database known as "with grant option".

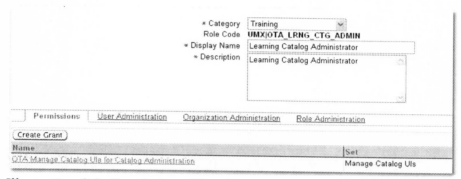

Illustration 2.2: Sysadmin > User Management > Roles and Role Inheritance: Role-characteristics

Role Categories

A labelling method which allows you to find your roles more easily. Make sure that you create easy to understand Role categories, like "HR", "Consultancy" or "DBA".

Permissions

Rights in OA_FRAMEWORK pages. These rights regard the screens that can be accessed (in the Set), the Data that can be used in the screen (Data Security) and Security Context (to which Responsibility the permissions apply). All actions concerning data security should be evaluated carefully.

Role Administration

A role which include role administration can be used for sub-administrator purposes (also known as local administrators). It allows you to grant and revoke the roles specified on the Role Administration sub-tab. (in database terms this is known as "with grant option"). *These are the roles a local administrator can give.*

User Administration

A local administrator must have User Administration Privileges to define which users he or she is allowed to manage. Local administrators can be granted different privileges for different subsets of users. For example, a local administrator can be granted privileges only to query one set of users, and granted full privileges (including update and reset password) for another set. Local administrators cannot query users if they don't have administration privileges for them. A local administrator with privileges is allowed to perform some specific actions on users such as reset passwords, grant or revoke roles of a user.

Organization Administration

Organization Administration Privileges define which external organizations a local administrator is allowed to view in Oracle User Management. This privilege enables an administrator to search for people within a organization, only if the local administrator has been granted privileges to view the people of that particular organization (User Administration Privileges). *These are the users on whom the actions can be performed.*

2.3. *Responsibilities for RBAC*

Oracle E-Business Suite provides three standard responsibilities for working with RBAC:
- Functional Developer
- Functional Administrator
- User Management

34

User Management covers all the functionalities, this is therefore recommended, but feel free to try the other responsibilities as well.

2.4. Enabling to work with RBAC

To be able to manage Roles, you have to work with the "User Management"-responsibility. Let's try it:
1. Assign your user the responsibility "User management".
2. Logout, and Logon again as this user
3. As you will see, you have the responsibility "User management"
4. Click on the responsibility "User Management". You have no screens in here. How is this possible?

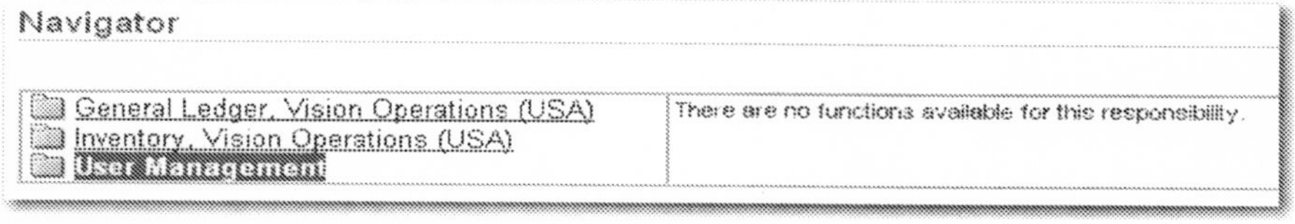

Navigator

General Ledger, Vision Operations (USA)   There are no functions available for this responsibility.
Inventory, Vision Operations (USA)
User Management

Illustration 2.3: User Management without the correct rights.

5. Go back to the responsibility System Administrator
6. Go to Responsibility, and search for the responsibility "User Management"
7. Search for the Menu that is linked to this responsibility (it is: "User Management : Top Level Menu")
8. Look for the menu details
9. As you will see, all the functions are not granted! This is the reason why you did not see the screens in your menu.
10. Logout and login as Sysadmin (Password sysadmin).
11. Click on the responsibility "User Management" and you'll see the User Management functions as follows:

Illustration 2.4: The functions of User Management.

12. Click on "Roles & Role Inheritance".
13. Search for your user and update it:

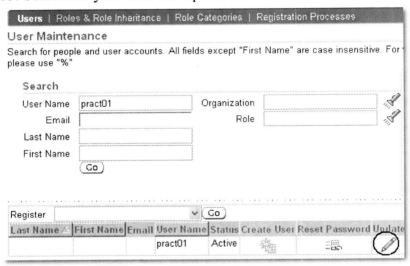

14. Click on "Assign Roles". Assign "Security Administrator". Fill in a justification (any will do). Logout and login as your user and test the responsibility "User Management".

Roles in Oracle E-Business Suite

Roles that are linked to a user are not visible in Core-eBS. But responsibilities that are inherited through a role are visible as Indirect Responsibilities:

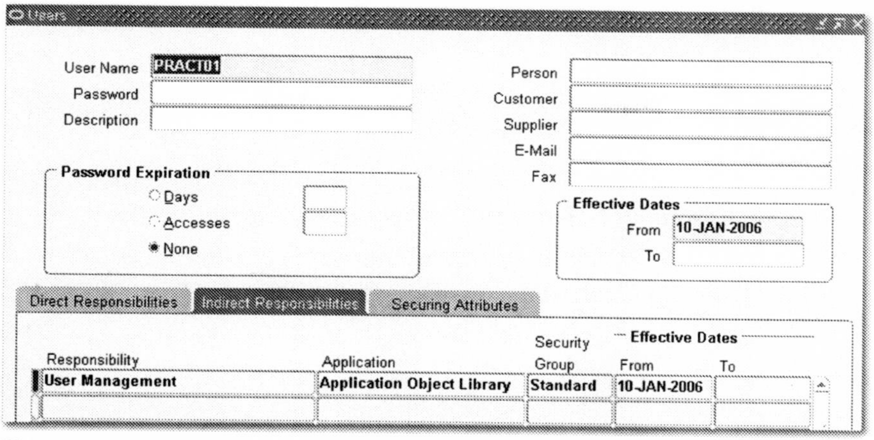

Illustration 2.5: A via a role inherited responsibility.

2.5. Guided exercise

Create a role and add two responsibilities to it

Create the role XXORG_GL_ROLE with two responsibilities: "General Ledger, Vision Banking, Analyst" and "Inventory, Vision Banking".

Step 1: Create a Role Category:

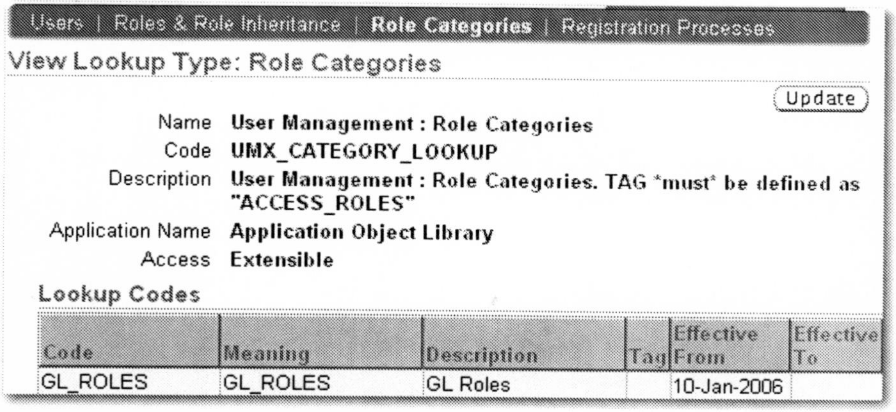

Illustration 2.6: First create a Role Category

Step 2: Create the new Role within this category: Role & Role Inheritance > Create Role:

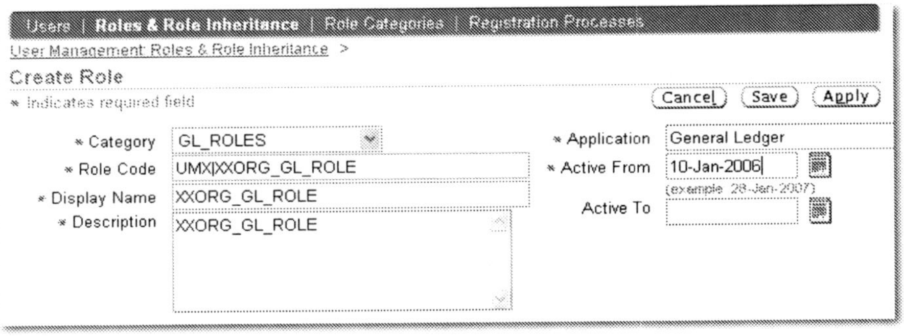

Illustration 2.7: A Role with the Role Category

Step 3: Role & Role Inheritance, search the tree for your Role, and click "Add Node":

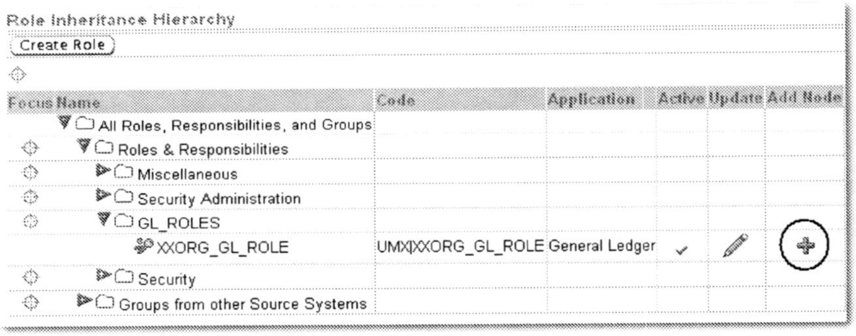

Illustration 2.8: Add a Responsibility to the Role

Step 4: Search for the Responsibility to add:

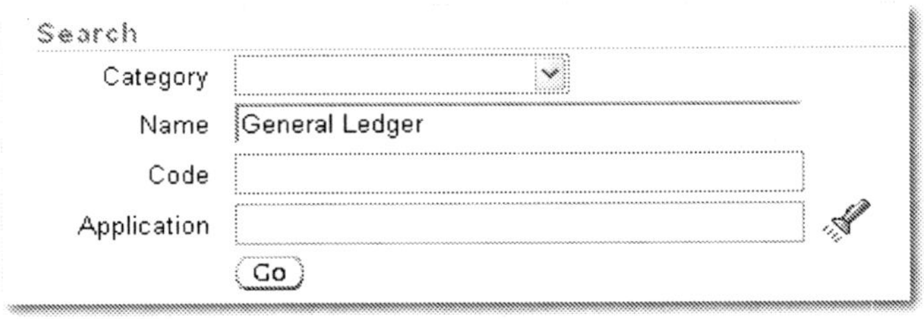

Illustration 2.9: Search for what to add to the Role

Step 5: Select "General Ledger, Vision Banking, Analyst".
Step 6: Expand the tree, and check that the responsibility has been added:

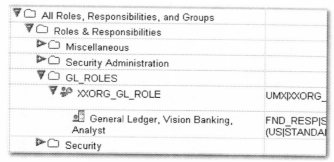

Illustration 2.10: The Responsibility is added to the Role

Tip: notice the symbol for a Role and the symbol for a responsibility.

Step 7: Add also the responsibility "Inventory, Vision Banking". Make sure to add this at the correct level:

Illustration 2.11: Also the Responsibility Inventory , Vision Banking is added

Create a user and give this user the above role.

Create user PRACT01_ROLE and assign to him the above role.
Step 1: In System Administrator, create user PRACT_ROLE:

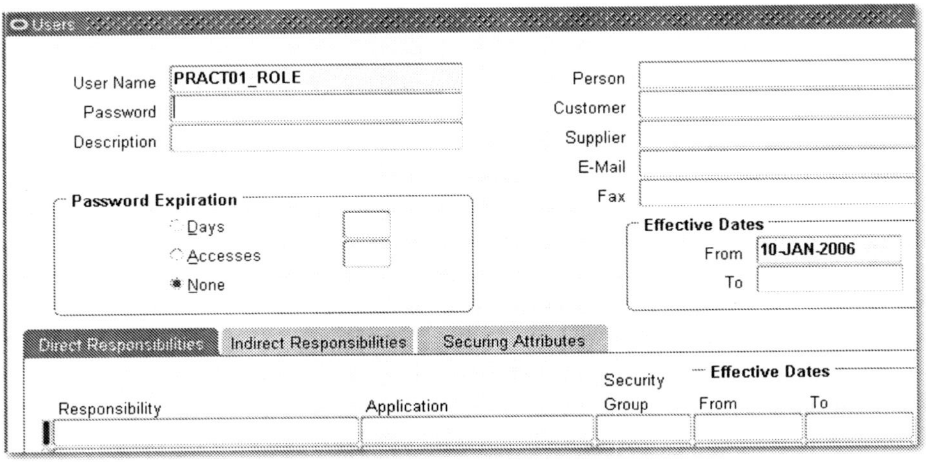

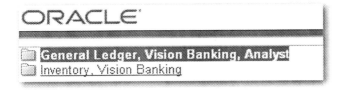

Users
User Name
PRACT01_ROLE
Password
Description
Person
Customer
Supplier
E-Mail
Fax
Password Expiration
Days
Accesses
None
Effective Dates
From
10-JAN-2006
To
Direct Responsibilities
Indirect Responsibilities
Securing Attributes
Responsibility
Application
Security Group
Effective Dates
From
To

Step 2: User Management > Users. Search for Pract01_role > update > Assign Roles:

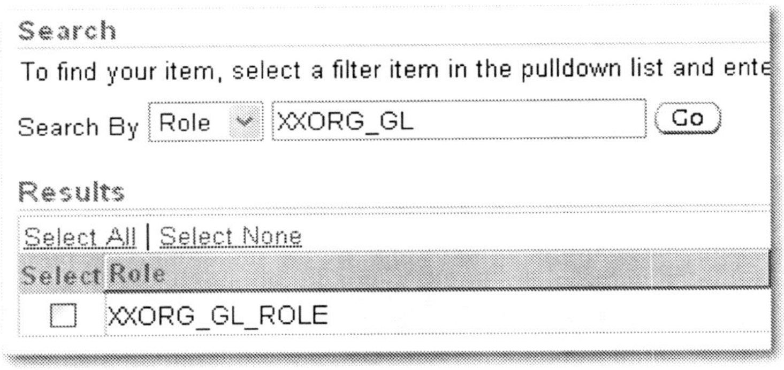

Search
To find your item, select a filter item in the pulldown list and ente
Search By
Role
XXORG_GL
Go
Results
Select All | Select None
Select
Role
XXORG_GL_ROLE

Illustration 2.12: Assign a Role to a User

Select and fill in a justification.

Step 3: To test it, login as this new user.

ORACLE
General Ledger, Vision Banking, Analyst
Inventory, Vision Banking

Add a role to a role

Add the role "Security Administrator" to the XXORG_GL_ROLE.
Step 1: User Management > Roles & Role Inheritance. Search for the XXORG_GL_ROLE and click "View in Hierarchy":

Search						
Type						
Name	XXORG_GL_ROLE					
Code						
Application						

Go

Create Role

Role	Code	Application	Active	View In Hierarchy	Update
XXORG_GL_ROLE	UMX|XXORG_GL_ROLE	General Ledger	✓		

Step 2: Click "Add Node" and search for the role that you want to add:

Search	
Category	
Name	Security Administrator
Code	
Application	

Go

Select	Quick Select	Role	Code	Application	Active
○		Security Administrator	UMX|SECURITY_ADMIN	Application Object Library	✓

Step 3: Select, logout and login as Pract01_role:

ORACLE

General Ledger, Vision Banking, Analyst	User Management
Inventory, Vision Banking	Users
User Management	Roles & Role Inheritance
	Role Categories
	Registration Processes

Delegated administration

Create a user XXGLSU who acts as a Local Administrator, and can assign the responsibility "General Ledger User".

1. Login as sysadmin / sysadmin, or any other user with the System Administrator responsibility.
2. Create the new user XXGLSU: click on the responsibility "System Administrator" > Security: User > Define. Give it the password: 12345 Link a person to this user.
3. Save and exit the core eBS environment.
4. Stay in the Framework environment.
5. Login as a user with User Management. Click on the responsibility User Management.
6. Click on Users.
7. Search for the user XXGLSU.
8. Click on the update icon at right-hand side of the user.
9. Assign the role: General Ledger Super User. (This could also have been done from within the Core-eBS environment).
10. Fill in the Justification: something like "needed for the exercises".
11. Click save.
12. Assign the role: Customer Administrator.
13. Again fill in a justification: something like "also needed for the exercises".
14. Click apply.
15. Click on the tab page "Roles & Role inheritance".
16. Search for the responsibility "General Ledger Super User".
17. Make sure that you work on the correct responsibility! Click the update link.
18. Click on "User Administration". Add the row with "All people", "All User Administration Privileges". Click Save.
19. Click on "Organization Administration", Add the row with "View all Organizations".
20. Click on "Role Administration". Select "Selected Row Below". And search for "General Ledger User". Move this one to the right. Click "apply".
21. Logout.
22. Login as XXGLSU / 12345. Change the password to "welcome".
23. Click on the responsibility "User Management". (Where does this responsibility come from?).

24.Search for your XXGLU user. Click the update link.
25.Click "assign role". As you can see, you can only link the "General Ledger User" responsibility to this person.
26.Logout.
27.Login again as sysadmin / sysadmin.
28.Click the responsibility "System Administrator" > Security: User > Define.
29.Search for your XXGLU user. As you can see, the responsibility has been added.

2.6. Exercises

1. Create a role XXORG_SU_## with the following responsibilities: "Payables, Vision Operations (USA)" and "Inventory, Vision Operations (USA)".
2. Add the role you have just created to your user.
3. Grant local administrator rights to the role you have just created, so that privileges for "Workflow User" and "Internet Time, Vision Utilities" can be granted.

2.7. Summary

This chapter was about using Roles to give rights to Users. It introduced you to the use of the responsibility "User Management", and its applications. In the guided exercises part we provided some examples on how to create a role, and work with delegated administration. At the end of this chapter you can find some exercises on the Role Based Access Control.

Chapter 3

Profiles

Sometimes computer systems have to be modified in order to be fine-tuned to your needs. Oracle E-Business Suite makes this possible thanks to its profiles. A profile is a set of changeable options that affect the way your application looks and behaves. Profiles can be set on various levels. Some can be set by the end-user and others can only be set by the System Administrator.

In this chapter, we'll start by analysing the actual possibilities given by these profiles. Then we'll continue with the profile levels, and provide you with a list of the most useful profiles. We will also discuss briefly how behaviour of profiles can be changed. Finally, you will be able to practice each of these topics with some specific exercises.

3.1. What are Profiles?

Profiles are settings in the eBusiness Suite. As for examples the settings:
- default printer
- number of copies
- how to display negative numbers etc.

3.2. What you can and cannot do with profiles

Profiles can do	Profiles cannot do
<ul><li>Change color of Core-eBS</li><li>change default printer</li><li>change logging-level</li><li>change time-out time</li></ul>	<ul><li>Change business flows (is done in Workflow)</li><li>change user rights (done in System Administrator)</li><li>change layouts of screens (done in Forms or OA-Framework Personalization)</li><li>send emails (done in Alert of Workflow)</li></ul>

Warning on changing profile values

Some of the profiles have a low impact, some other may affect heavily the way the suite runs.

Rule 1: never change a profile if you don't know its function.

Rule 2: let the functional administrator set the profiles for his / her application (this means that the General Ledger administrator sets the profiles for GL).

Rule 3: be aware that for some profile changes you may have to login again for them to have effect. The name of the profile does not tell you if this is the case.

3.3. Profile Types

Since 11.5.10 Oracle E-Business Suite has three types of profiles:
- security profiles
- organization profiles

- server profiles

In previous versions, only the security profiles existed.

Security Profiles

Despite the name, security profiles can be used for all kinds of purposes: for setting your default Printer, for formatting issues and indeed also for security purposes like AuditTrail.

Organization Profiles

Organization profiles are useful for Multi-Org purposes in order to set profile values for a certain Operating Unit.

Server Profiles

Server profiles are used when the behavior of Oracle eBS depends on the middle tier it is running. Server Profiles are used for handling Cookies, or for handling PLSQL Web Agents.

3.4. The setting levels of security profiles

These profiles can normally be set on four levels:

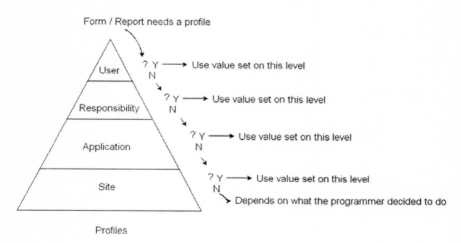

3.5. The setting levels of organization profiles

These profiles can normally be set on three levels:

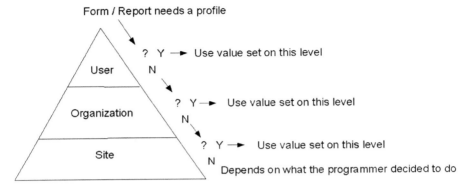

3.6. The setting levels of server profiles

These profiles can normally be set on three levels:

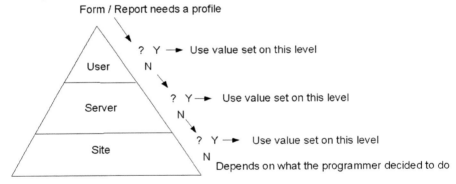

3.7. What makes a profile a security, an organization or a server profile?

This is established in the profile definition. This definition can be viewed (and changed) via the responsibility "Application Developer":

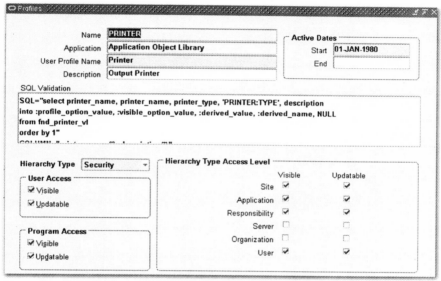

Illustration 3.1: Application Developer > Profile

In the dropdown List box "Hierarchy-type" on the left side you can define the type of the profile. Here you can make the profile Visible and Updatable for the user. The Hierarchy Type Access Level indicates that a System Administrator can set and view this profile on Site, Application, Responsibility and User level.

3.8. Personal Profiles and System Profiles

Personal profiles can be set by the user using the Menu-option Profile > Personal or selecting Preferences > Profiles from the Edit menu:

Illustration 3.2: Setting of User Profiles

System profiles can only be set by a System Administrator.

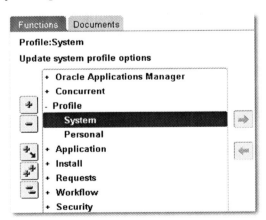

Illustration 3.3: Setting of System Profiles

50

Personal Profiles can be set, of course, only on user level. System Profiles can be set on all levels.
When querying the System Profiles for your profile, all the data regarding user, responsibility and application should be entered.

Modifying the protection level of a profile

In case you are not happy about the settings of a profile, and, as system administrator, you want to turn a personal profile to a system profile, then you have to use the responsibility "Application Developer". This responsibility allows you to define the the profiles behaviour.

3.9. Setting System profiles at Site level

Since release 11.5.10, for security reasons, it is no longer possible to set profiles at site level. If you try this, you'll get the error message:

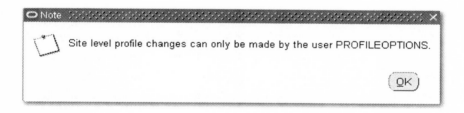

A way around this, is to ask for the password of the user PROFILEOPTIONS, and try it again. Another option (hack) is to disable the customization made on this screen as follows: from the Help menu select Diagnostics > Custom Code > Off.

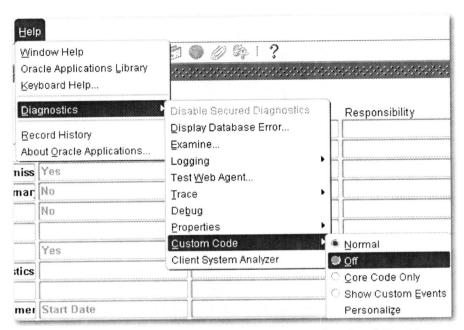

Illustration 3.4: Set Custom Code Off for setting Site level Profiles

Then you will be asked to enter the Oracle password (this is the password of the Apps-account on the database, for a Vision environment, the password = apps).

3.10. A list of useful profiles

Profile	Purpose
Look-and-Feel	
Java Color Scheme	Change the color of Core-eBS
Java Look and Feel	Windows95 interface or Oracle interface
Currencies	
Currency:Negative Format	How to display a negative currency in a screen or report
Currency: Thousands Separator	, / .
Folder: Allow Customization	Can a user modify a Folder?
Concurrent Requests	
Concurrent: Request Priority	Set Priority level for example in printing documents
Concurrent:Save Output	Always save a copy of a report
Concurrent:Attach URL	For sending the URL of the request to the requester by mail
Concurrent: Show Requests Summary After Each Request Submission	After request submission, the Request Summary screen is shown immediately
Concurrent:Hold Requests	New requests are put on hold
Concurrent:Report Copies	Default number of copies
Personalization	
Personalize Self-Service Defn	For allowing OA-Framework personalizations
FND: Personalization Region Link Enabled	Enables to customize the Region link
Disable Self-service Personal	If set on Site level, no personalizations will be shown. This is needed in case personalizations corrupt the suite
FND: Branding Size	To set the size of the logo on Framework pages
Self Service Personal Home Page	For a old (11.5.9) or new (Framework) login page
Site Name	The name of the machine as displayed in the Title-bar of main window

Profile	Purpose
Flexfields	
Flexfields:Shorthand Entry	For the use of aliases in Flexfields
Flexfields:Open Descr Window	Descriptive Flexfield is opened when clicked
Flexfields:Open Key Window	Key Flexfield is opened when clicked
Security	
Sign-On: Notification	Lists number of open notification on login
Sign-On: Audit Level	Logging level (on Form level)
AuditTrail: Activate	Start auditing on data level
ICX: Limit time	maximum duration (in hours) of a user's session
ICX: Session Timeout	the length of time (in minutes) of inactivity in a user's session before the session is disabled.
Hide Diagnostics menu entry	Hides the Diagnostics menu
Utilities:Diagnostics	Makes it possible to go in the Diagnostics > Examine screen without password
Multi-Org	
MO: Operating Unit	Sets the Operating Unit
HR: Business Group	Defines HR Business Group
GL: Set of Books Name	The General Ledger Set of Books
Login-screen	
Local Login Mask	Include several optional attributes in the login page
Printer	
Printer	Change the default printer

3.11. Guided Exercise

Display Username and Password Hint

The Profile 'Local Login Mask' has several attributes with a value:
- Username Hint = 01

- Password Hint = 02
- Cancel Button = 04
- Forgot Password Link = 08
- Register Here Link = 16
- Language Images = 32
- Sarbanes Oxley Text = 64

If a client wanted to display the password hint and forgot password attributes on the login page, then the profile value should be set to 10 (02+08). In order to display just the language images, set the profile value to 32, which is the default.

Step 1: Logout, and see how the login-screen looks:

Step 2: Login as Operations, go to the System profiles, and query for Local Login Mask. The value is 32, which means that the Languages Images should be displayed. But if only one language is installed, no language image is displayed. Since we also want to display the Password Hint, the new value should be $32 + 2 + 1 = 35$.

Step 3: Switch off the System Profile security, as explained on page 51. Re-open the System Profiles screen, and set the value for the Profile to 35:

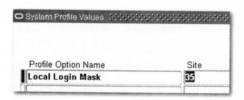

Step 4: Logout. Refresh the login-screen. If the screen does not look different, the problem may be caused by caching. Open a new browser.

3.12. Documentation resources on profiles

All the user guides can be found on the Oracle documentation site[1]. Most user guides include extended information on profiles. For example, the Oracle Assets User Guide dedicates nine pages on profile options. The Oracle General Ledger User Guide includes a whole chapter on the GL Profiles:

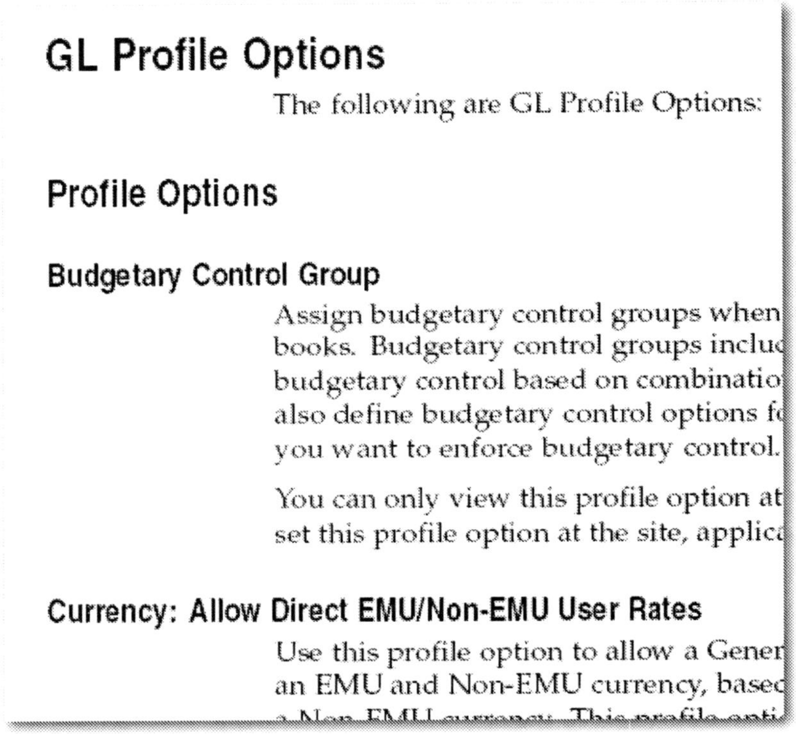

GL Profile Options

The following are GL Profile Options:

Profile Options

Budgetary Control Group

Assign budgetary control groups when books. Budgetary control groups includ budgetary control based on combinatio also define budgetary control options f you want to enforce budgetary control.

You can only view this profile option at set this profile option at the site, applic

Currency: Allow Direct EMU/Non-EMU User Rates

Use this profile option to allow a Gener an EMU and Non-EMU currency, based

Illustration 3.5: GL-profiles as described in the General Ledger User Guide

---

1   http://www.oracle.com/technology/documentation/applications.html

3.13. Exercises

1. Change the color of Core-eBS for your user to Blue.
2. Set the number of copies for your GL responsibility to 2.
3. Give the names of two server profiles.
4. Give the names of two organization profiles.
5. At which level can an administrator set the profile "FND: Log Mode"?
6. What does GL profile "GL AHM: Allow User to Modify Hierarchy" do?

3.14. A final tip

As you might have noticed, searching for a profile and its meaning is not too difficult. However, knowing which profiles are available in the system can give some problems. Therefore, it is a good practice for Functional Administrators to read the manuals of each new release, focusing particularly on the profiles part.

3.15. Summary

This chapter explained the purpose of profiles, and described the three main profile types, how to set a profile and modify its protection level. We provided also some information on reference material and some exercises.

Chapter **4**

Concurrent Programs

Besides data entry (entering and querying data through the screens), you also might want to print some reports of the data contained in the system. Since an Oracle system can be very large, calculating and printing the data can take quite some time. In the meantime you probably want to continue working on the data entry while the system is running your report. To allow all this to happen simultaneously, Oracle uses Concurrent Programs.

In this chapter we'll look how you can run (request) a program with parameters and how the administrator can administer (stop, cancel) requested programs. We'll also take a glance at Coded Request Groups, which is a security extension and later at the Request Sets.

4.1. What are Concurrent Programs?

Concurrent Programs are programs that can run simultaneously. They run in the background. This is also called batch processing.

4.2. Standard Request Submission: SRS

If you want a report to be printed, you have to submit a request.

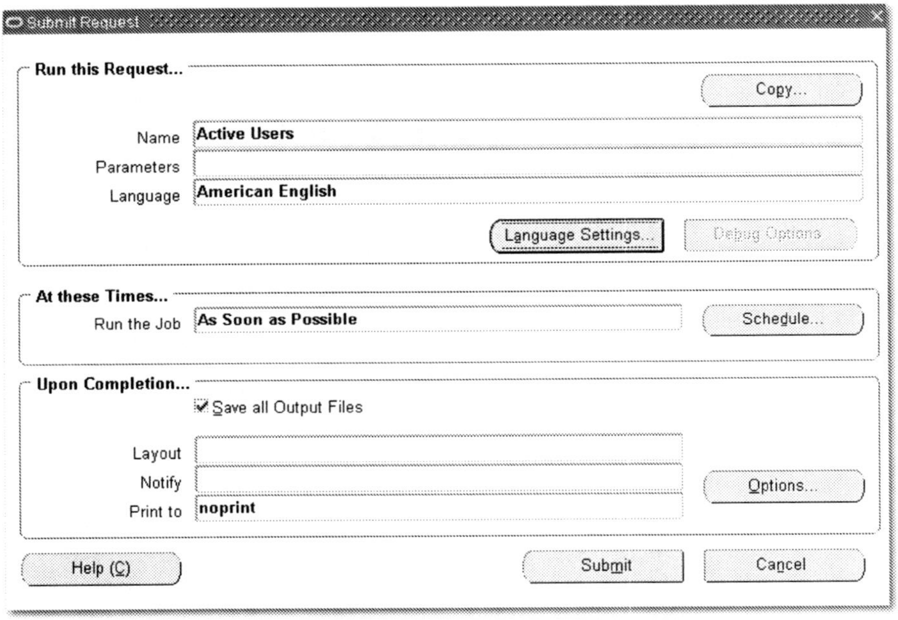

Illustration 4.1: System Administrator > Request > Run > Single Request

Most of the options of the Submit Request screen speak for themselves. After pressing "Submit", you can go to the View Requests screen, and press "Find" to check the status of your request.
After a while, the status changes from "Pending" to "Running" and then to "Completed".

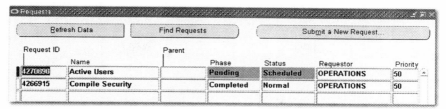

Request ID	Name	Parent	Phase	Status	Requestor	Priority
4270890	Active Users		Pending	Scheduled	OPERATIONS	50
4266915	Compile Security		Completed	Normal	OPERATIONS	50

Illustration 4.2: System Administrator > Request > View

If the Request is completed, you can click "View Output", to view the report in your browser:

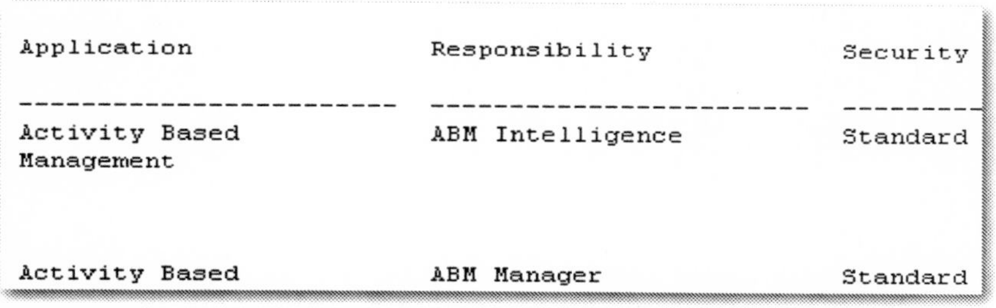

Application	Responsibility	Security
Activity Based Management	ABM Intelligence	Standard
Activity Based	ABM Manager	Standard

Illustration 4.3: Output of a Report

The Request is submitted and handled as illustrated below:

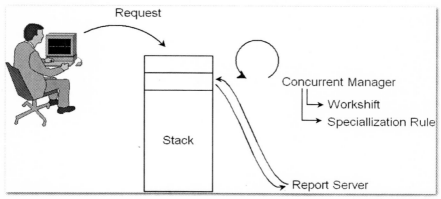

Illustration 4.4: The request of a user is read from a table (stack) and passed to the Report Server.

The concurrent Manager passed the Request to the Report server.

Concurrent Managers are described in chapter 5, starting on page 77. Normally a Concurrent Program is a Report or a (purge) script. Be aware of what you are running! You can easily drop all kinds of data, and a report can run for a very long time.

In Illustration 4.4 we see:

1. a user requesting a report, via Request > Run
2. the request is placed on the stack (a table in E-Business Suite) and that is also committed.
3. a concurrent manager that is running (based on the work shift) queries on the stack and 'gives' the programs he can start (based on the specialization rules) to the report server.
4. the report server executes the report and sets the status to 'Running' and later to 'Completed' on completion of the report.

Reprinting a report

If the output of a report is saved to the file system (this is an option when you request the report, or can also be done via profile: "Concurrent: Save Output"), then you can also reprint the report. The output, placed on the file system, is then directly send to the printer. In this way the report does not have to be recalculated.

Place on Navigator

If a request is completed, it can be placed on the navigator:
As a result, the request is placed also on the Document-tab page:

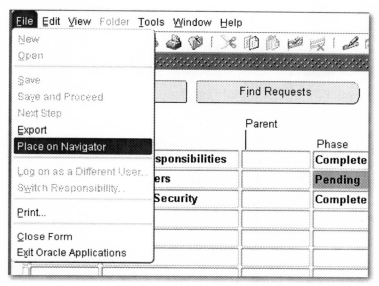

Illustration 4.5: System Administrator > Request > View > Place on Navigator

By clicking on it, the Request-View screen automatically opens with this request. This makes it easy to bookmark and find your important requests.

Canceling a Request

If a request is not running yet (is scheduled), the administrator can cancel the request by going to the Cancel Request screen: System Administrator > Request > View > Cancel Request.
If it is a repeating request, all requests will be canceled.

Placing a request on Hold

Same as for Canceling a Request:

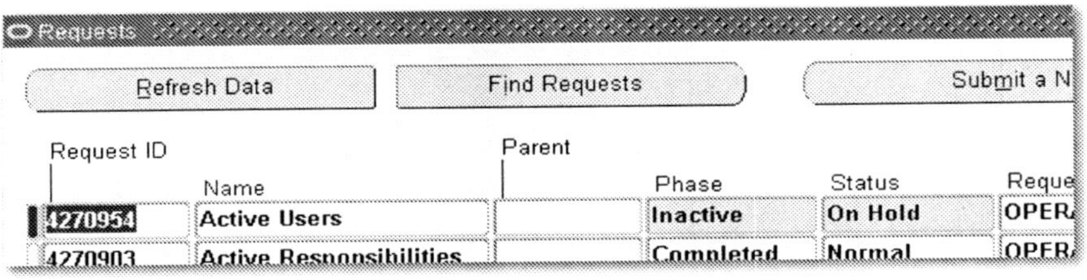

Illustration 4.6: A Request that is placed on hold.

However, this is something temporary: as long as the request is on hold, it will not be started. This makes it possible to do some maintenance on the file system of the Report server. Placing a request on hold can be done by hand or via the profile "Concurrent: Hold Requests".

The log-files

The View Requests screen includes also a button for the log files. Select a completed request and click on "View Log..". This is particularly useful if an error had occurred.
Log files can take a lot of space on the mid-tier, and therefore they must be deleted regularly. It is recommended use the option "Purge Concurrent Request and/or Manager Data" in the Concurrent Request screen. This program does three things:
- it removes the log files of the Concurrent programs
- it removes the log files of the Concurrent Managers (these can be found in System Administrator > Concurrent > Manager > Administer > select a manager > press "Processes" > "Manager Log"
- it removes the Request entries in the Requests View table

Report Output in Word

In a default installation, reports are shown in the browser (see Illustration 4.3). If you want to see your report in Word, the administrator can set the MIME-type linked to the report-output type:

64

PostScript	▾	application/postscript	Browser
RTF	▾	application/rtf	Microsoft Word
Text	▾	application/msword	Microsoft Word
Text	▾	text/plain	Notepad
XML	▾	text/xml	Browser

Illustration 4.7: System Administrator > Install > Viewer Options

This means that a text report is recognized on the Client as a application/msword or a text/plain document. Depending on your eBS-version you have to restart the Concurrent Manager that handles your requests (see Chapter 5, it is likely to be the Standard Manager).
Run the request and click "View Output". You now get to choose the application you want to use to open the report:

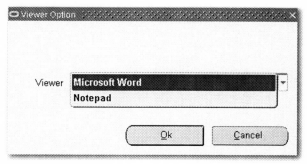

Illustration 4.8: Requests > View > View Output

Depending on the MIME type handling of your browser, the report will either open as a Word doc:

```
Page        1

Application                      Responsibility
User                            Start           End


------------------------        ------------
------------------------        ------------    ------
00 Custom                       00 CUSTOM DBI
```

or the browser will ask what to do, so that it can be downloaded as a Word document:

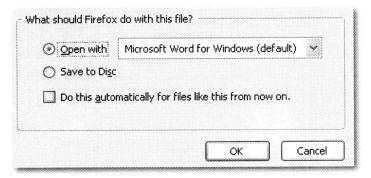

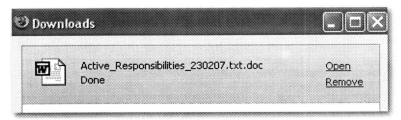

4.3. Request Sets

A Request Set is a group of Requests that is requested as a group. This can useful for example in the following situations:

- if at the end of the week you always run 5 reports, so this becomes one request
- if you wish to run several reports, but not at the same time. This can be achieved using stages.

Stages

A Request Set works with stages. Programs inside a stage can run at the same time (parallel), but all programs of a stage must be completed before going to the next stage (sequential). In the case illustrated in the picture below, Request A and B can run at the same time, or A can be completed before B, or vice versa. However, only when both A and B have been completed, Request C can start.

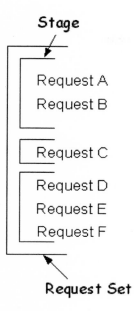

Illustration 4.9: A
Request Set with
stages.

Passing parameters

Parameters can be passed among Requests in a Request Group. This is useful if you have to pass parameters like a date, a period, a Set-Of-Books. Passing the parameter will prevent errors.

4.4.   Coded Request Groups

A coded request group is a group of requests that can be linked to a menu through a Function. The main advantage for the user is that the selection of the programs is much easier. For more reference, see also the Guided exercise below.

4.5. Guided exercises

Schedule a repeating program

Schedule the program "Active Users" to run every week on Friday.
Step 1: Login with a user with the System Administrator responsibility.
Step 2: Request > Run > single request. Select "Active Users" and click "Schedule". Fill in the parameters:

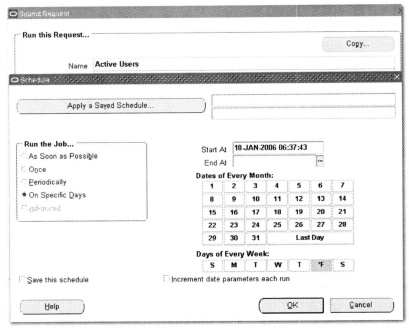

Illustration 4.10: A repeating Concurrent Program.

Step3: Click "Ok", and then click "Submit".

Create a Request Set with parameter passing

Create a Request Set with two requests in it: "Purge Obsolete Workflow Runtime Data" and "Purge Concurrent Request and/or Manager Data". These two requests may run at the same time. And you must pass a parameter for the number of days (since this is used in both requests).

Step 1: Go to System Administrator > Requests > Set, and make a new Request Set:

Illustration 4.11: System Administrator > Requests > Set. Save.

Step 2: Click "Define Stages": make just one stage, since the programs can run together:

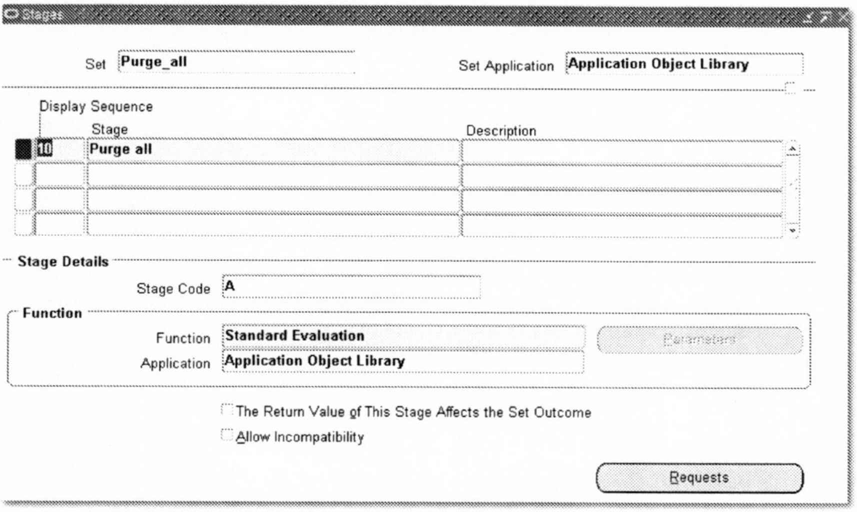

Illustration 4.12: Stage definition in the Request Set.

Step 3: Click "Requests", to enter the Programs in the Stage:

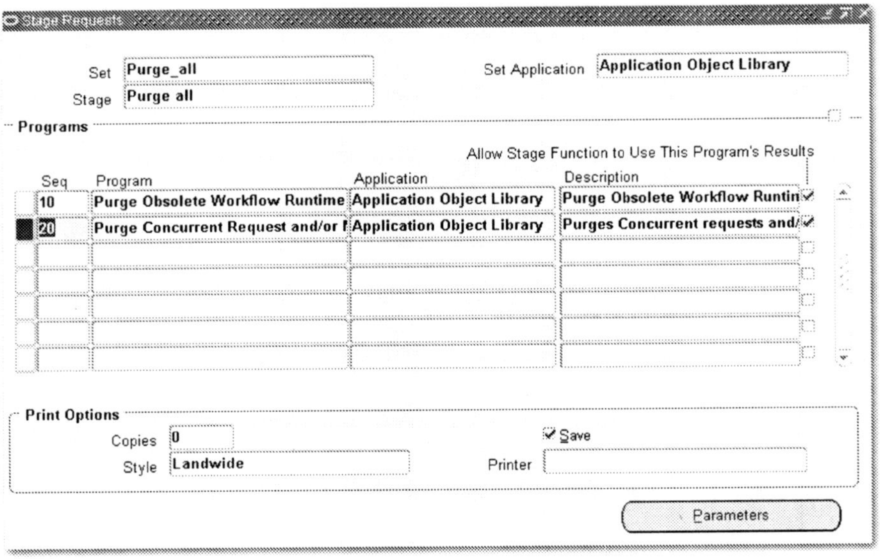

Illustration 4.13: The Programs in the Stage.

Step 4: Save. Select "Purge Obsolete Workflow Runtime Data" and click "Parameters". Enter the circled values. DAYSOLD is just an example.

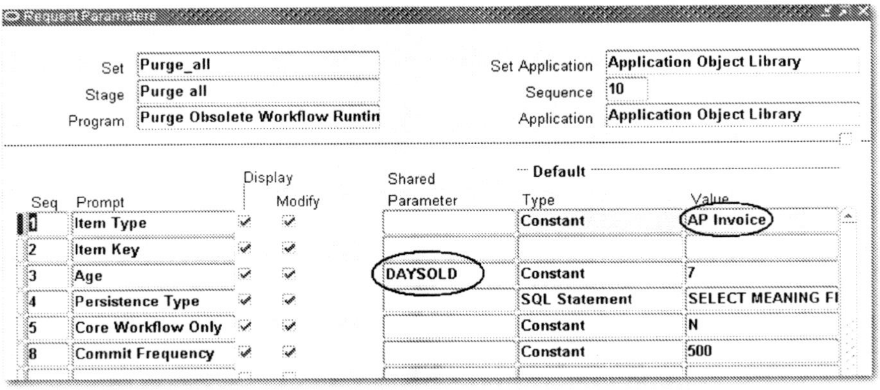

Illustration 4.14: Parameters of the Request. DAYSOLD is a shared parameter.

Step 5: Save, close the screen, and open the parameter screen for the "purge Concurrent Request and/or Manager Data" and enter a parameter:

Illustration 4.15: Entering the parameters for the second request.

Step 6: Link the stages. Save, close all the screens until you get to the Requests Set main screen of. Click on "Link Stages":

Step 7: Fill in the stages:

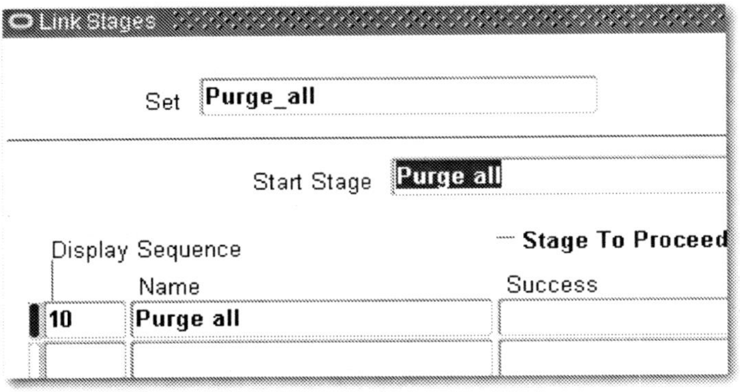

Illustration 4.16: Only one stage to be linked.

Step 8: Save and close. Add the Request Set to your Request Group, and test it: Requests > Run > Request Set. Select your Request Set and fill in the parameters for the first Request:

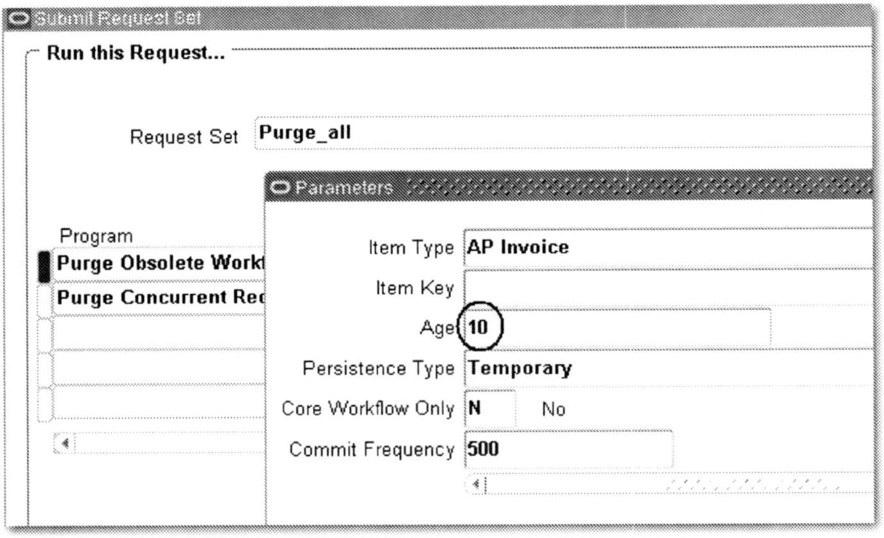

Illustration 4.17: The parameters screen. Item Type has a default, Age is changed to 10.

Step 9: Click "OK" and open the parameters for the second Request. You will see that the parameter DAYSOLD is passed automatically:

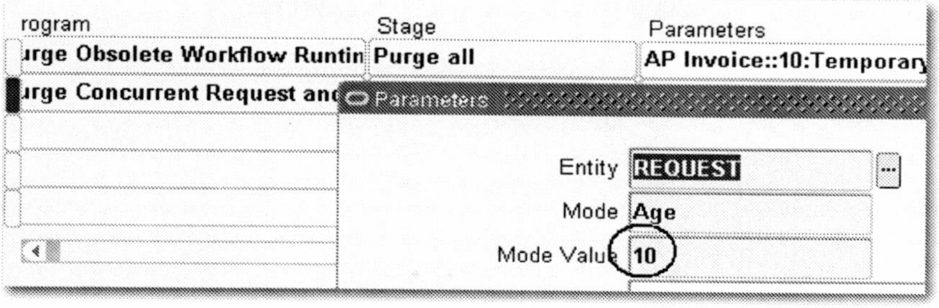

Illustration 4.18: The passed parameter.

Step 10: Test if it works then you may also delete it.

Create a coded Request Group

Create a Coded Request Group, with programs need to be run each month, and add it to your System Administrator Responsibility.

Step 1: Create the relative Request Group, and of course enter the code:

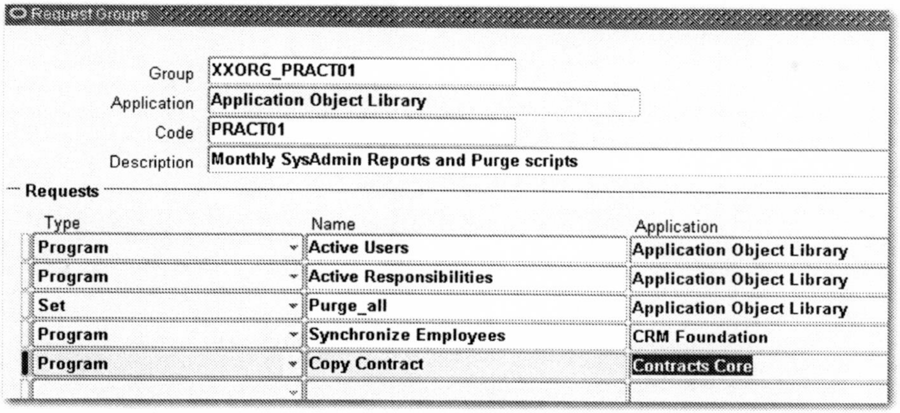

Illustration 4.19: Security > Responsibility > Request

Step 2: Create a Function which links to this Request Group:

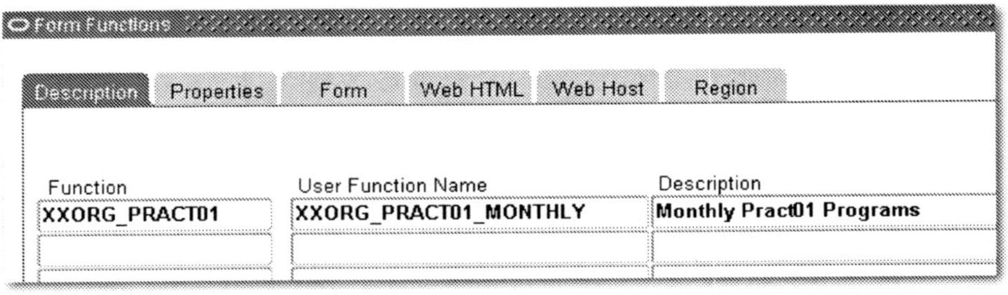

Form Functions
Description
Properties
Form
Web HTML
Web Host
Region
Function
XXORG_PRACT01
User Function Name
XXORG_PRACT01_MONTHLY
Description
Monthly Pract01 Programs

Illustration 4.20: System Administrator > Application > Function

Step 3: Enter Form under Type:

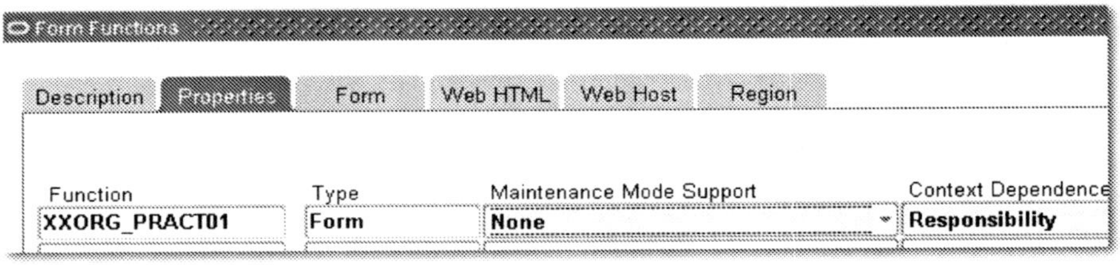

Form Functions
Description
Properties
Form
Web HTML
Web Host
Region
Function
XXORG_PRACT01
Type
Form
Maintenance Mode Support
None
Context Dependence
Responsibility

Step 4: Fill in the remaining fields. Please see below how to fill in the parameters field:

Form Functions
Description
Properties
Form
Web HTML
Web Host
Region
Function
XXORG_PRACT01
Form
Run Reports
Application
Application Object Lib
Parameters
Editor
TITLE="PRACT01 Programs"
REQUEST_GROUP_CODE="PRACT01"
REQUEST_GROUP_APPL_SHORT_NAME="FND"
OK
Cancel
Search

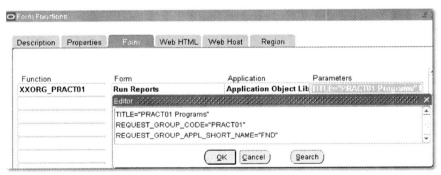

Illustration 4.21: The parameters of the Coded Request Group

Step 5: Add it to your menu and test it. You'll see the Requests that have been added to the group:

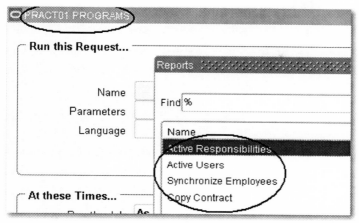

Illustration 4.22: Result of the Coded Request group.

4.6. Exercises

1. In your System Administrator responsibility request the program "Report Group Responsibilities". It must run every two hours for four hours long, starting at midnight.
2. Create a Request Set with two programs that cannot run at the same time. The programs are "Accounting Rules Listing Report" and "ACE Non-Depreciating Assets Exception Report". Pass parameters if possible, and give some parameters a default value. Test if you can start the Request Set and can pass parameters, if applicable. The programs do not need to be run.
3. Create a coded Request Group with the two programs mentioned above so that you can run them separately. Add the coded Request Group to your user with restricted rights, and test it.

4.7. Summary

This chapter explained how to manage Concurrent Programs. It explained the advanced features of the Coded Request Group and the Request Set. This chapter provided also some exercises on Concurrent Programs.

Chapter 5

Concurrent Managers

Normally a system can easily manage long running reports. However, when your system is heavily loaded, reports or programs requiring a lot of processing may slow down the system severely. In such a case, it is possible for the user to schedule the program to run during night time, but as administrator you may want such programs to run always during the night or in the weekend. For this purpose, Oracle E-Business Suite provides administrators with Concurrent Managers that can take care of load balancing.

In this chapter we'll deal with Concurrent Managers and explain how to create, administer them and set their parameters. Then we will provide some explanations on specialization rules and work shifts and end with some exercises on Concurrent Managers.

5.1. What are Concurrent Managers?

Concurrent Managers are processes which run on the mid-tier and pass requests to the Report Server. Instead of running the report themselves, they pass the request with all its parameters to the Report Server. This means that if Concurrent Managers are down, no reports will be printed, since nothing has been passed to the Report Server.

5.2. Types of Concurrent Managers

The ICM It is the Internal Concurrent Manager, which acts as the "boss" of all the other managers. The Internal Concurrent Manager starts up,resets, shuts down and verifies the status of individual managers.

The Standard Manager

The Standard Manager is a normal manger. It runs always (work shift = 24 * 7) and has no specialization rule, which means that this manager can start all programs.

The Conflict Resolution Manager

Concurrent managers read requests and start concurrent programs. The Conflict Resolution Manager checks concurrent program definitions for incompatibility rules.

If a program is identified as Run Alone, then the Conflict Resolution Manager prevents the concurrent managers from starting other programs in the same conflict domain.

When a program lists other programs as incompatible, the Conflict Resolution Manager prevents these program from starting until the execution of incompatible programs in the same domain has been completed.

5.3. Defining a Concurrent Manager

As depicted in illustration 4.4 on page 61 the concurrent managers query the requests and pass their data to the Reports Server (or PLSQL-engine depending on the request type). If a concurrent manager is not running, the request will just be waiting on the stack. This is used for load-balancing. Requests that require a lot of CPU should be forced to run during night time. To achieve this, you need a new Concurrent Manager with a work shift during the night and a specialization rule that includes only this specific Request.

The Concurrent Manager screen

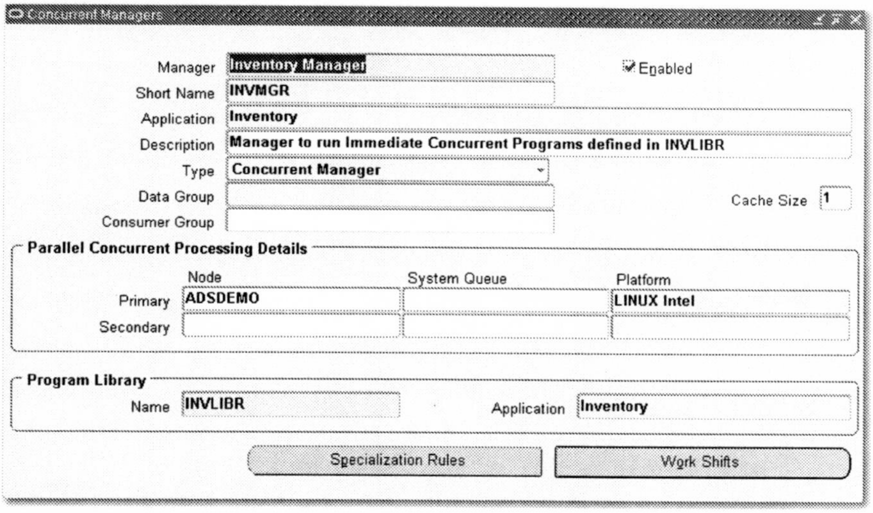

Illustration 5.1: System Administrator > Concurrent > Manager > Define

In this screen you can define the Concurrent Managers. You must link predefined Work shifts and link Specialization Rules to it to make Load balancing possible.

Work Shifts

A work shift indicates when the Concurrent manager is running. A Concurrent manager can have several Work shifts. In the Work shifts screen you can create work shifts for later use.

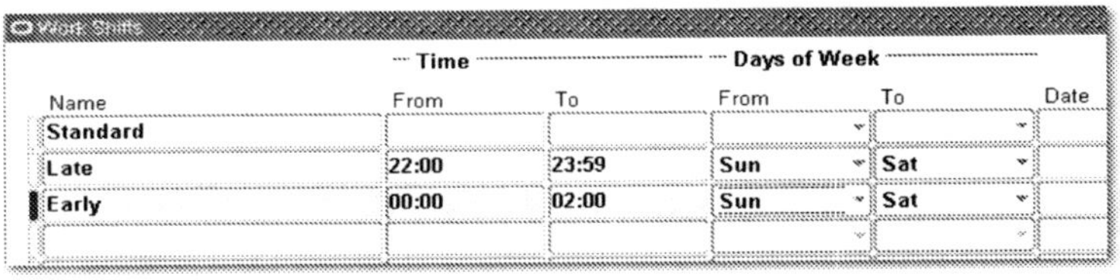

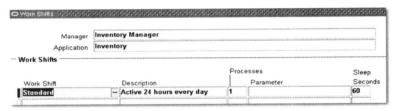

Illustration 5.2: System Administrator > Concurrent > Manager > Work Shifts

If you press on the "Work Shifts" button (on illustration 5.1) you'll see the actual Work shift(s) attached to the Inventory Manager:

Illustration 5.3: A Work shift attached to a Manager.

Specialization Rules

A specialization rule defines what a Concurrent Manager is allowed or or not allowed to start. Specialization Rules for the Inventory Manager are:

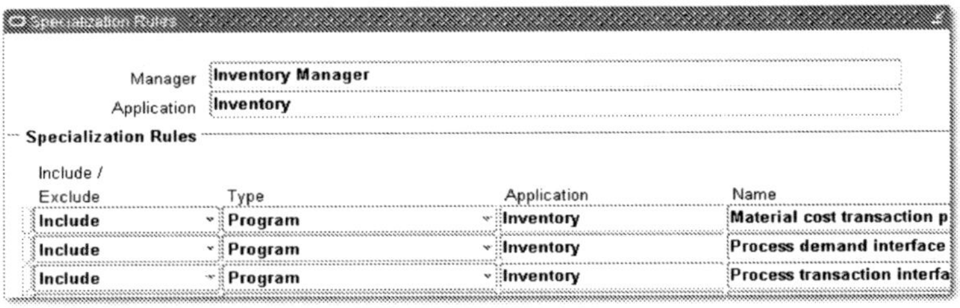

Illustration 5.4: The Specialization rules for the Inventory Manager.

80

In this case, this manager has only include-rules. An exclude rule includes all the rest, therefore, this manager can run only the given programs.

Note: Include and exclude rules should never be mixed. So, you should only use include or only exclude rules.

Consumer Groups

Consumer Groups have been introduced in 11.5.8, and you can see them in illustration 5.1. If you click on the Consumer Group, you see a screen representing the Resource Consumer Groups as defined by the database administrator in the database:

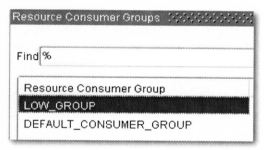

Illustration 5.5: The Resource Consumer Group belonging to the Concurrent Manager.

Through the Resource Consumer Groups you can increase or decrease the CPU time or the number of IO actions allowed to the Concurrent Manager. In this way your programs can actually run faster, since they may get more CPU-time.

In case the standard solution of Oracle for scheduling does not deliver enough flexibility, there are commercial add-ons for scheduling on the market[2].

---

2   http://www.appworx.com/

5.4. Administering the Concurrent Managers

Concurrent Managers can be started, deactivated etcetera in the Administer Manager screen:

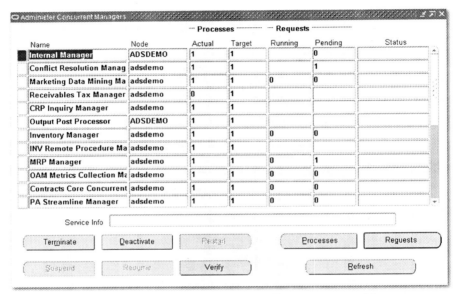

| Name | Node | Processes | | Requests | | Status |
		Actual	Target	Running	Pending	
Internal Manager	ADSDEMO	1	1		0	
Conflict Resolution Manag	adsdemo	1	1		1	
Marketing Data Mining Ma	adsdemo	1	1	0	0	
Receivables Tax Manager	adsdemo	0	1			
CRP Inquiry Manager	adsdemo	1	1			
Output Post Processor	ADSDEMO	1	1			
Inventory Manager	adsdemo	1	1	0	0	
INV Remote Procedure Ma	adsdemo	1	1			
MRP Manager	adsdemo	1	1	0	1	
OAM Metrics Collection Ma	adsdemo	1	1	0	0	
Contracts Core Concurrent	adsdemo	1	1	0	0	
PA Streamline Manager	adsdemo	1	1	0	0	

Service Info

[Terminate] [Deactivate] [Restart]   [Processes] [Requests]

[Suspend] [Resume] [Verify]   [Refresh]

Illustration 5.6: System Administrator > Concurrent > Manager > Administer

Warning!!

Never terminate or deactivate the Internal Manager. If the ICM goes down, all other managers will go down as well, and as a result, no one in your organization will be able to print, or purge. Besides, this manager can be started only with a Unix command, and not through the standard screen.

Terminate

It stops the manager and kills all running processes. Not recommended.

Deactivate

It stops the manager, and gives all the running processes time to finish.

Restart

It restarts the manager. Can take two or three minutes.

Processes

You will see two columns labeled 'Actual' and 'Target'. The Target column lists the number of processes that should be running for each manager for this particular work shift. The Actual column lists the number of processes that are actually running. If the Actual column is zero, there are no processes running for this manager. If the Target column is zero, then either a work shift has not been assigned to this manager, or the current work shift does not specify any target processes. If the target column is not zero, then the manager processes have either failed to start up, or gone down. You should check the manager's log file.

5.5. Guided exercises

Starting and Stopping a Manager

Stop the "PA Streamline Manager" and start it again.
Step 1: Go to the Administer Concurrent Manager screen, select the "PA Streamline Manager", and click on "Deactivate". The status should change to "Deactivating".
Step 2: After a couple of minutes, the status should be "Deactivated".
Step 3: Press now "Activate" and the status should change to "Activating". After about three minutes, the status should be empty again, which means everything is running properly.

5.6.   Exercises

Use simple load-balancing. You must create a new Concurrent Manager, that runs from 23.00 – 03.00 h, and starts only the programs described in the exercises on page 29. Or, in case you haven't done your exercise, make sure you select a program that you can run in your responsibility. Make sure that the program cannot run during the daytime (hint: do not forget the Standard Manager).
Request the program to run as soon as possible, and check that it does not start. Also check tomorrow whether your program has been executed.

5.7.   Summary

In this chapter we discussed the creation and administration of Concurrent Managers. We have dealt in particular with work shifts, and their role in load-balancing. We have provided some practical examples on Concurrent Managers and some exercises on load-balancing with the Concurrent Managers.

Chapter 6

Printers

Reports can only be printed to a printer that is registered to the Oracle E-Business Suite.

This chapter will give you some general guidelines on how to register a printer in the E-Business Suite without being too specific. For further information you can always refer to the Technical Reference Manual.

6.1. The Printer screens

Style

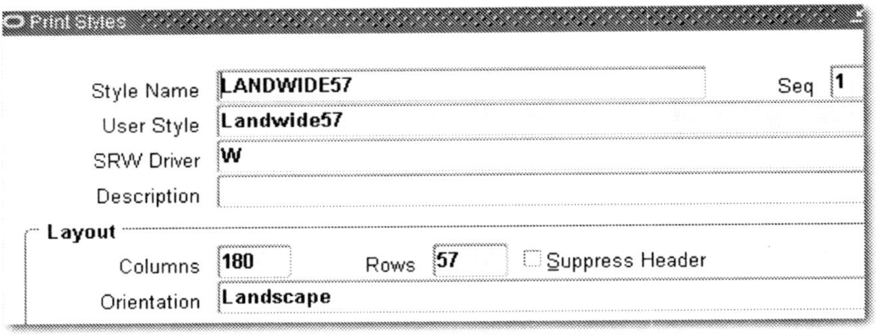

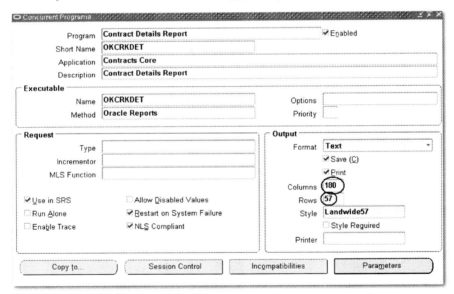

Illustration 6.1: *System Administrator > Install > Printer > Style*
A lot of Printer Styles are predefined. You should not change them, since they fit the size of Oracle's shipped reports:

Illustration 6.2: *System Administrator > Concurrent > Program > Define*

Driver

The drivers are platform specific drivers for printers:

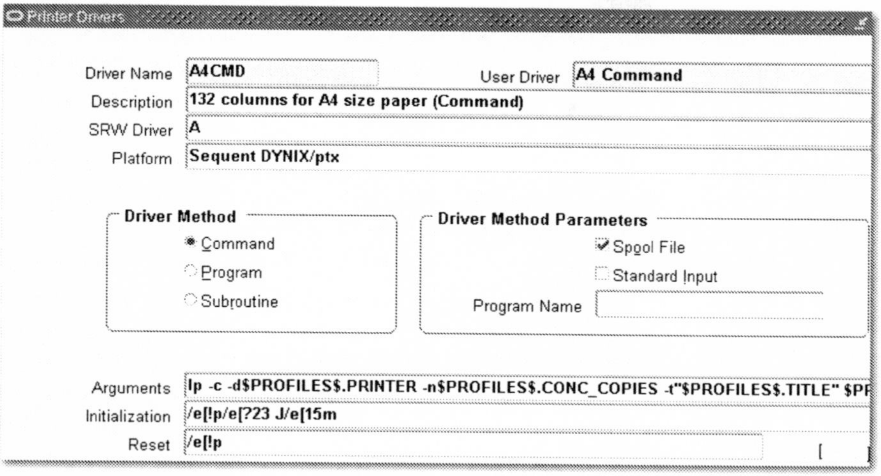

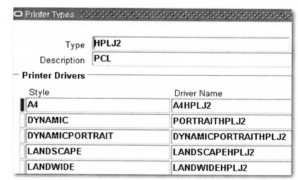

Illustration 6.3: System Administrator > Install > Printer > Driver

In illustration 6.3 you can see the SRW-Driver, SRW stands for SQL-Report Writer. This is an old technique for Oracle Reports. It is a formatting file, not a real driver. You can also see the Unix/Linux commands: lp -c ...

Types

A type is a predefined printer with the drivers and the styles it can print.

Printer Types	
Type	HPLJ2
Description	PCL

Printer Drivers

Style	Driver Name
A4	A4HPLJ2
DYNAMIC	PORTRAITHPLJ2
DYNAMICPORTRAIT	DYNAMICPORTRAITHPLJ2
LANDSCAPE	LANDSCAPEHPLJ2
LANDWIDE	LANDWIDEHPLJ2

Illustration 6.4: System Administration > Install > Printer > Types

Register

Printer	Type	Description
LabelPDF	Label	PDF Printer for WMS Labels
LoftwareLPS	Label	Loftware LPS Printer - Please Assign IP
Zebra	Label	Zebra Label Printer
adsprinter	HPLJ4SI	PCL
noprint	HPLJ4SI	

Illustration 6.5: System Administrator > Install > Printer > Register
Most of the times this is the screen that really matters. The name of the
printer must be the name of the Print Queue. The screen does not
perform any check on the availability of this print queue.

6.2. After installation: restart the Concurrent Managers

After installation, the Concurrent Managers (see Chapter 5) must be
restarted. Otherwise the Concurrent Programs (see Chapter 4) will not
be able to use the new printer, and all kinds of errors will occur.
Normally, a system administrator will add a printer to the system and
will make the printer available to the users for the next day.

6.3. Pasta Printer

In Oracle E-Business Suite R11.5.9 a new printer type called Pasta
Printer has been added. Its driver automatically converts text files
(output of most reports) to Postscript. This is useful, because you can
link all postscript printers to Oracle E-Business Suite without having
to install all different kinds of drivers.

Why is it already (almost) outdated

At the moment, Oracle is focusing mainly on BI-Publisher, a tool
integrated in Oracle E-Business Suite. BI-Publisher converts XML

output (possible from most reports) to pdf. For this reason the pasta driver is not really needed anymore.

6.4. Security with Printers

The administrator can define to which printer a report must be sent for printing:

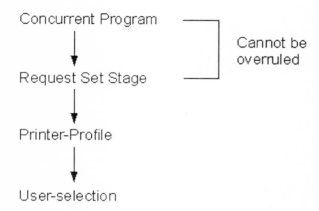

Illustration 6.6: The printer selection scheme

In the Concurrent Program you can define which printer should print it. If this is not defined, it will take the default printer set in the Request Set Stage (if the user prints a Request Set):

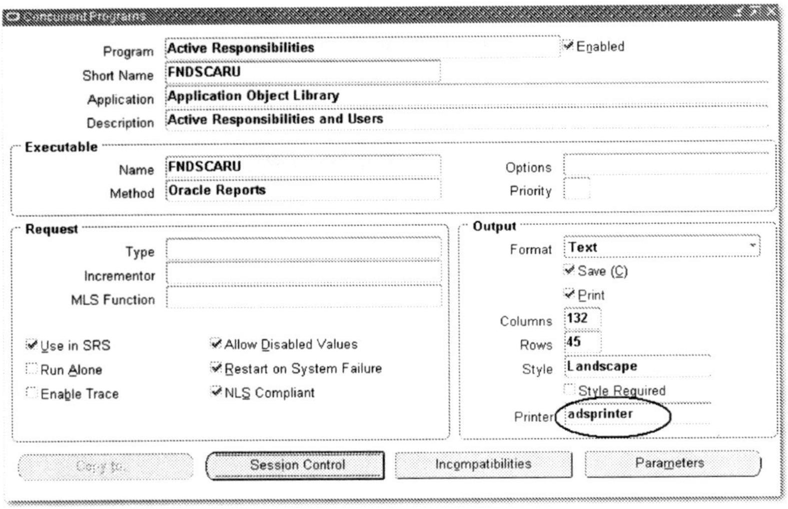

Illustration 6.7: System Administrator > Concurrent > Program > Define

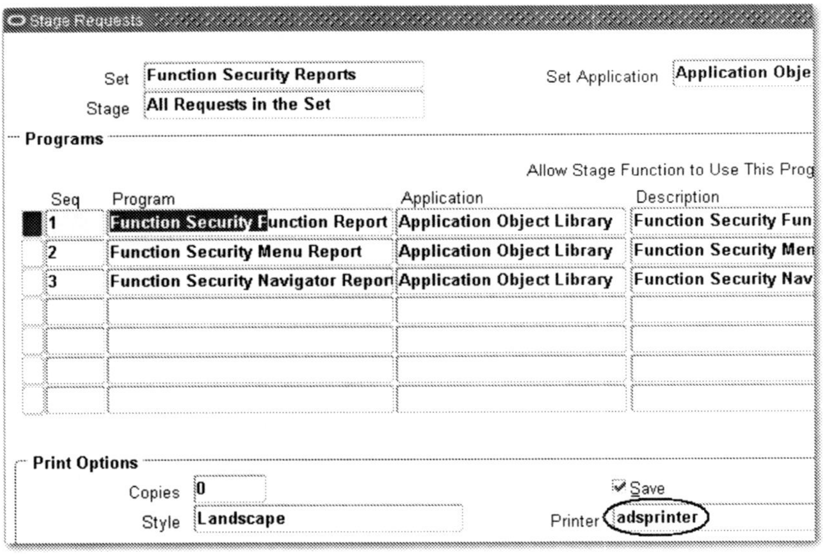

Illustration 6.8: system Administrator > Requests > Set

If this is empty it will look in the user's Printer profile, and if this is also empty, it will ask for any printer to print it.

6.5. Exercises

Exercising on printers is quite difficult since:
- a change in printers will only be active after restarting all Concurrent Managers
- a new Printer must have a working Print Queue, otherwise the exercises will result in all kind of errors

1. Modify program "Concurrent Program Details Report" so that it will be only printable on a specific printer.
2. Modify the program so that the output cannot be saved. Test it. Does this really work?

6.6. Summary

This chapter dealt with the installation and registration of printers to the eBusiness Suite. Some important points were made in particular with regard to security.

Chapter 7

Forms Personalization

The forms in the Oracle E-Business Suite look simply awesome. But still, there might be situations when you or a colleague would like to have a field disabled or a prompt changed. Especially when changing a screen can really improve productivity. To make this possible, and easy to maintain, in the version 11.5.10, Oracle introduced Forms Personalization.

In this chapter you'll learn how to work with Forms Personalization, and how to administer the changes you have made. We will give a brief overview of the advantages, possibilities and limitations of form personalization and provide several demonstrations and provide some exercises for further practice.

7.1.   What is Forms Personalization?

Forms Personalization is a technique which allows you to modify Core-eBS (Forms based screens) without having to work with Oracle Developer, or having to access the mid-tier. The personalizations are patch-proof, which means that after an upgrade or patch, your modifications will still be in place.

7.2.   Three ways to modify a Core-eBS screen

Change the fmb file

Changing the *fmb* file is far the most powerful way to modify a screen. You will have all the possibilities available in Forms: from making a field mandatory to adding and removing tab pages and sub-forms.
Advantages:
  • offers as much possibilities as Oracle Forms
Disadvantages:
  • you need access to the mid-tier
  • changes made are standard not patch-proof (they can be made patch-proof, though)
  • a good knowledge of Oracle Forms is required

Change the Custom.pll file

All forms in Oracle E-Business Suite are linked to a *Custom.pll* file. You can modify the properties of a form directly in this file, without actually changing the form.
Advantages:
  • patch-proof
  • knowledge of Oracle Forms is not necessary
  • easier than changing the *fmb* file
Disadvantages:
  • you still need access to the mid-tier
  • limited possibilities: new fields, tab pages etcetera cannot be made
  • difficult to maintain

Work with Forms Personalization

Forms Personalization is in fact a change in the Custom.pll file which is entered through a normal screen. This mechanism has been introduced in release 11.5.10.

Advantages:
- easier than changing the Custom.pll
- easy to maintain
- no access to the mid-tier needed
- patch-proof

Disadvantages:
- limited possibilities: new fields, tab pages etcetera cannot be made

Which technique should you choose?

When you need to add fields, you must change the *fmb* file. In all other cases: use Forms Personalization.

7.3. What is possible with FP

You can change properties of fields and tab pages: prompt, tool tip, visibility, changeability, layout, default values.
You can display pop-up messages.
You can add menu-entries to the form.
You can use standard Forms Build-ins, like GO_BLOCK, FND_FUNCTION.EXECUTE.

7.4. What is not possible with FP

You cannot create new objects on the screen. Besides, if the customizations you are creating interfere with the form, in some cases they will be overruled / overwritten and therefore not shown. You cannot say beforehand in what cases your personalization will be overwritten. Just try it, and you'll see it.

7.5. Security settings

Two profiles (described on page 54) are useful here:

Profile	Purpose
Hide Diagnostics menu entry	Hides the Diagnostics menu
Utilities:Diagnostics	Makes it possible to go in the Diagnostics > Examine screen without password

You should normally set the profile "Hide Diagnostics menu entry" to Yes for all normal users, and set this profile to No for those who are going to make Forms Personalizations.
The profile "Utilities: Diagnostics" should be set to Yes for the persons who are going to make Forms Personalizations, and to No for everybody else.

7.6. How Forms Personalization works

Go to the screen that you want to modify. Let's say we want the Responsibilities screen to be modified.

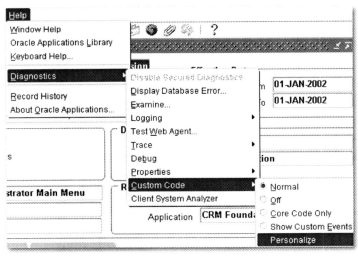

Illustration 7.1: Opening the Forms Personalize-option in the screen that you want to modify.

Forms Personalization works with Rules, Triggers, Conditions and Actions. They are related as follows:

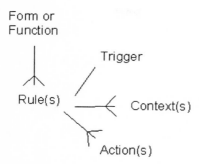

Illustration 7.2: The components of a Forms Personalization.

Form or Function

Form means: the modification is done on this fmb. Function means: it is done on this function only, if the form is also used in another function, then the modification is not shown.

Rule

The name of the modification that you want to make.
Tip: give it a clear name like "Disable fields", since this is what later will appear in Administration screen.

Trigger

Indicates when the modification will be executed. Example: directly (WHEN_NEW_FORM_INSTANCE), or when you jump to another block (WHEN_NEW_BLOCK_INSTANCE).

Context

Who will see the modification? Can be User, Responsibility, Site or Industry (these are verticals like Oil & Gas).

Action

What kind of actions can be done? Possible choices: change a *Property* (field color), add a *Message* (pop-up), execute a *Build-in* (GO_BLOCK) and add a *Menu* (in the Form).

7.7. Forms Personalization Administration

In the Forms Personalization screen the administrator can disable rules.

Illustration 7.3: Administrators can disable Rules.
As you can see, choosing a clear name for your rules might be of great help for the administrator.

7.8. Copying Personalizations from Test to Production

Once you create and test personalizations in your test instance, you can move them to production instances. Personalizations are extracted by the loader on a function basis (i.e. each loader file will contain all personalizations for a single function).

Note: Upon uploading, all prior personalizations for that function will be deleted, and then the contents of the loader file will be inserted.

The loader syntax is as follows:
Download:
FNDLOAD <userid>/<password> 0 Y DOWNLOAD
$FND_TOP/patch/115/import/affrmcus.lct <filename.ldt>
FND_FORM_CUSTOM_RULES function_name=<function name>
Function_name is a required parameter; if it is not supplied, no personalizations will be downloaded.
Upload:
FNDLOAD <userid>/<password> 0 Y UPLOAD
$FND_TOP/patch/115/import/affrmcus.lct <filename.ldt>

7.9. Guided exercises

Add tool tips

Add a tool tip to the responsibility key field indicating that this is used for FND*Load.

Step 1: Open the Responsibilities screen, and go to Help > Diagnostics > Custom Code > personalize.

Step 2: Enter data for the Rule, Trigger and Context:

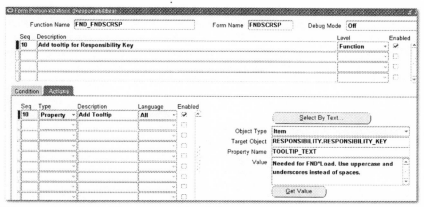

Function Name FND_FNDSCRSP	Form Name FNDSCRSP	Debug Mode Off

Seq	Description	Level
10	Add tooltip for Responsibility Key	Function

Condition | **Actions**

Trigger Event WHEN-NEW-FORM-INSTANCE (You can enter additional event names.)
Trigger Object
Condition

Processing Mode Not in Enter-Query Mode
Context
Level Value
User OPERATIONS

Illustration 7.4: The condition and context for the personalization.

Step 3: Enter the action:

Function Name FND_FNDSCRSP	Form Name FNDSCRSP	Debug Mode Off

Seq	Description	Level	Enabled
10	Add tooltip for Responsibility Key	Function	☑

Condition **Actions**

Seq	Type	Description	Language	Enabled
10	Property	Add Tooltip	All	☑

Select By Text...

Object Type Item
Target Object RESPONSIBILITY.RESPONSIBILITY_KEY
Property Name TOOLTIP_TEXT
Value Needed for FND*Load. Use uppercase and underscores instead of spaces.

Get Value

Illustration 7.5: The action(s) of the personalization.

Step 4: Save, close the screen and re-enter the screen:

Responsibility Name	**(Obsolete) CRM Administrator, Vision**
Application	**CRM Foundation**
Responsibility Key	**JTF_ADMINISTRATOR_TM**

Needed for FND*Load. Use uppercase and underscores instead of spaces.

Available From ————————————— Data Group ————

Illustration 7.6: Testing of the personalization.

Make a field mandatory

Make the Request Group field mandatory.
Step 1: Make a new rule, Trigger =
WHEN_NEW_FORM_INSTANCE, Context = User, action:

Function Name	FND_FNDSCRSP	Form Name	FNDSCRSP	Debug Mode Off

Seq	Description	Level	Enabled
10	Add tooltip for Responsibility Key	Function	✓
20	Make Request Group Mandatory	Function	✓

Condition | **Actions**

Seq	Type	Description	Language	Enabled			
10	Property	Make Mandatory	All	✓		Select By Text...	
20	Property	Tooltip for ReqGrou	All	✓	Object Type	Item	
					Target Object	RESPONSIBILITY.REQUEST_GROUP_NAME	
					Property Name	REQUIRED	
					Value	TRUE	

Illustration 7.7: One rule with two related actions.

Step 2: Save, close the screen and re-enter the screen:

Request Group	
Name	**CRM Administration**
Application	**Request Group is always needed.**

Illustration 7.8: Field is mandatory and has a tool tip.

Remove a field

Same as the above examples, except that the Property Name = Displayed.

Change a prompt for a specific responsibility

Again, the same as above, but in this case the Context is now Responsibility (and of course, you have to indicate for which responsibility the personalization is shown) and Property Name = Prompt_Text.

Link a report to a screen

Link the report "Active Responsibilities" to this screen.
Step 1: Make a new Rule. With Trigger = WHEN_NEW_FORM_INSTANCE with Context = User.
Step 2: Enter data for the Action. We have to make a Menu entry (Special 1-15 becomes "Tools"-menu, 16-30 becomes "Reports"-menu, 31-45 becomes "Actions"-menu):

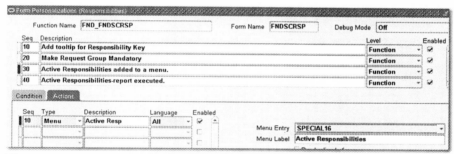

Illustration 7.9: Making the menu-entry.

Step 3: Make a new Rule, with Trigger = SPECIAL16 (means: if this menu option is pressed), and action.
Step 4: Save, close the screen and re-enter the screen to test it.

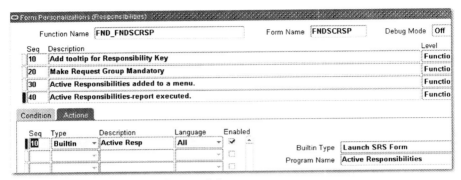

Illustration 7.10: The calling of the report.

Make (parts of) a screen read-only

Same as the above examples, make property "Enabled" false.

Give a Field conditionally a default

Make the Effective To-Date equal to the current date + 1 month, if the Responsibility name starts with XXTMP.

Step 1: make a new Rule with a conditional trigger:

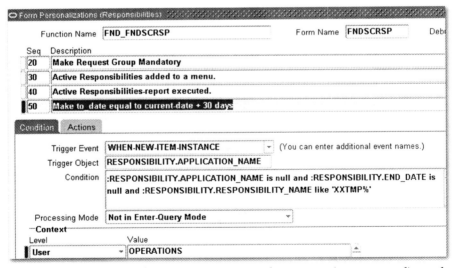

Illustration 7.11: Application name must be empty (new record), end-date must also be empty and responsibility must start with XXTMP.

Step 2: Enter data for the Action:

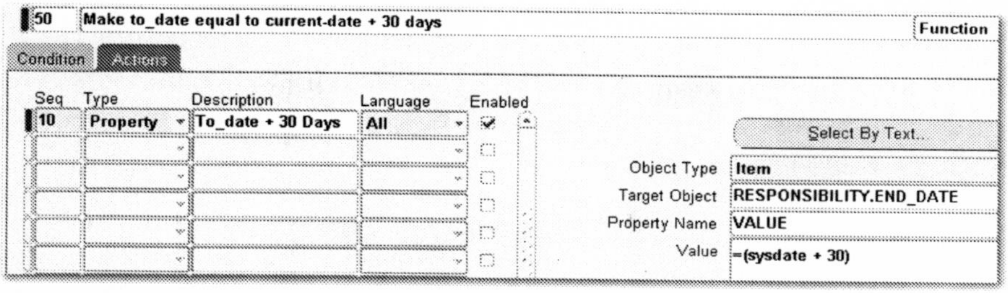

| 50 | Make to_date equal to current-date + 30 days | | | | | | Function |

Condition   **Actions**

Seq	Type	Description	Language	Enabled	
10	Property ▾	To_date + 30 Days	All ▾	☑	
	▾		▾	☐	
	▾		▾	☐	
	▾		▾	☐	
	▾		▾	☐	
	▾		▾	☐	

Select By Text..

Object Type : Item
Target Object : RESPONSIBILITY.END_DATE
Property Name : VALUE
Value : =(sysdate + 30)

Step 3: Save, close the screen and re-enter the screen to test it.
Step 4: Improved Action:

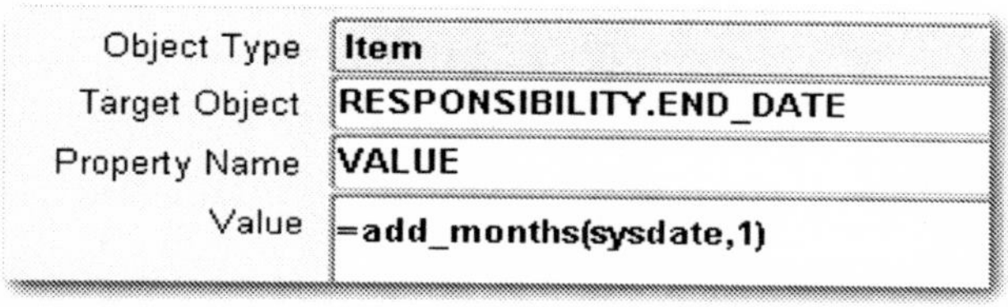

Object Type	**Item**
Target Object	**RESPONSIBILITY.END_DATE**
Property Name	**VALUE**
Value	**=add_months(sysdate,1)**

Illustration 7.12: SQL functions are allowed in actions and conditions.

Make a zoom to another screen

Make a zoom from the Responsibilities screen to the Menus screen.
Both the Responsibility and the Menu screen must be personalized.
Step 1: Make a zoom menu:

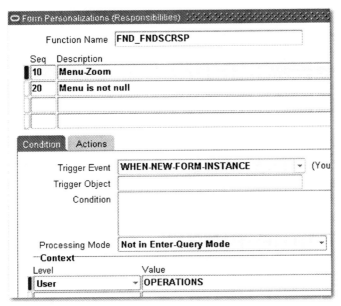

Illustration 7.13: Make the rule for the menu-entry.

Step 2: Enter data for the Actions:

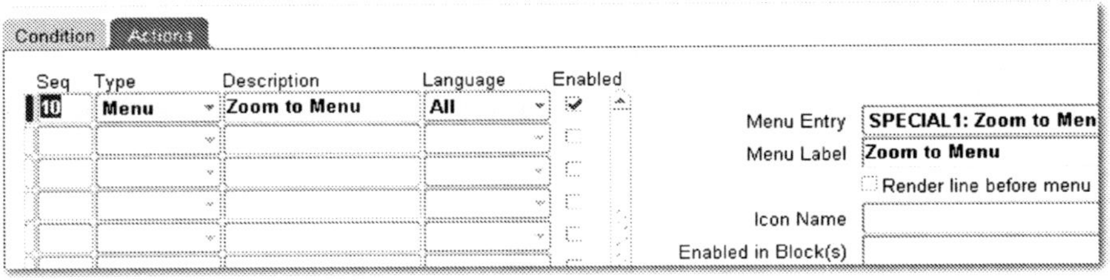

Illustration 7.14: Add the menu, and give it a label.

Step 3: Only zoom if the menu field is not empty:

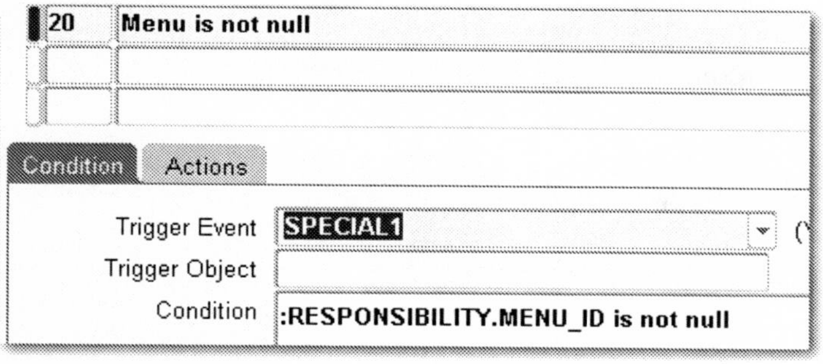

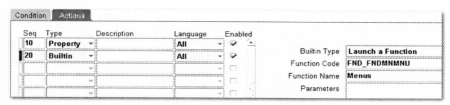

20	Menu is not null		

Condition   Actions

Trigger Event	**SPECIAL1** ▾
Trigger Object	
Condition	:RESPONSIBILITY.MENU_ID is not null

Illustration 7.15: Check if you must zoom.

Step 4: Enter data for the two Actions. First enter a Global variable:

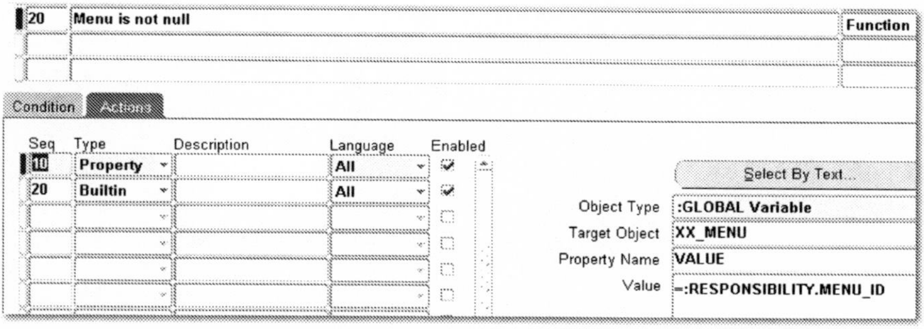

20	Menu is not null		Function

Condition   **Actions**

Seq	Type	Description	Language	Enabled		
10	Property ▾		All ▾	☑	▲	
20	Builtin ▾		All ▾	☑		
	▾			☐		Object Type :GLOBAL Variable
	▾			☐		Target Object XX_MENU
	▾			☐		Property Name VALUE
						Value =:RESPONSIBILITY.MENU_ID

Select By Text...

Illustration 7.16: Fill the global. It is created automatically.

Then call the builtin:

Condition   **Actions**

Seq	Type	Description	Language	Enabled	
10	Property ▾		All ▾	☑	▲
20	Builtin ▾		All ▾	☑	
	▾			☐	
	▾			☐	

Builtin Type	**Launch a Function**
Function Code	FND_FNDMNMNU
Function Name	**Menus**
Parameters	

Illustration 7.17: Call the function of the menu screen.

Step 5: In the Menu screen: Personalize the Menu screen. We will create three rules. The first rule is to create a Global variable (1 action), the second rule goes to the correct block and in enter-query mode (two actions), and the third rule fills the query field, executes the query and makes the global empty (three action). Make a new rule to create the Global variable:

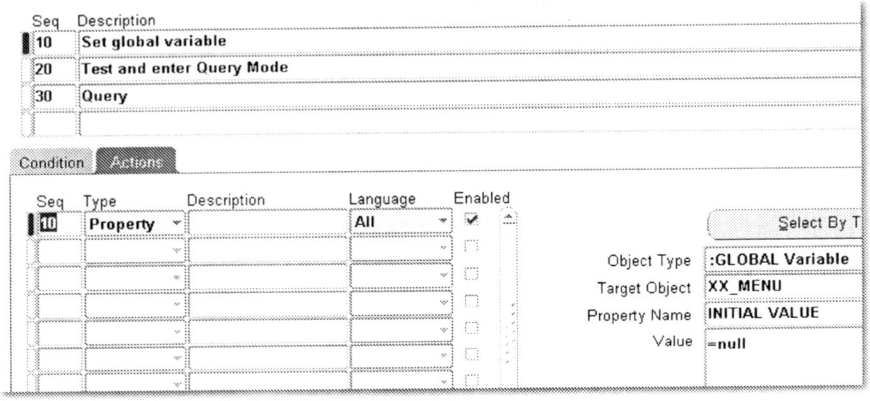

Illustration 7.18: Create a global-variable in the Menu-screen.

Step 6: Test if the Global variable is filled in a new Rule. Don't do the action in the Query mode:

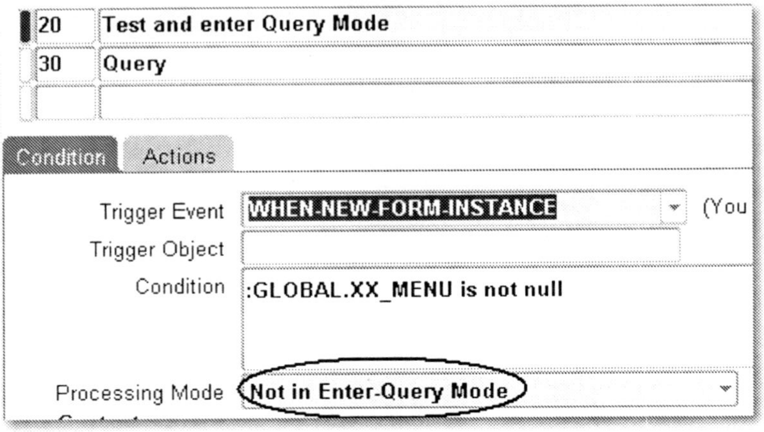

Illustration 7.19: Don't work with the global if the screen is already in Enter-Query mode.

Step 7: Add actions to this rule:

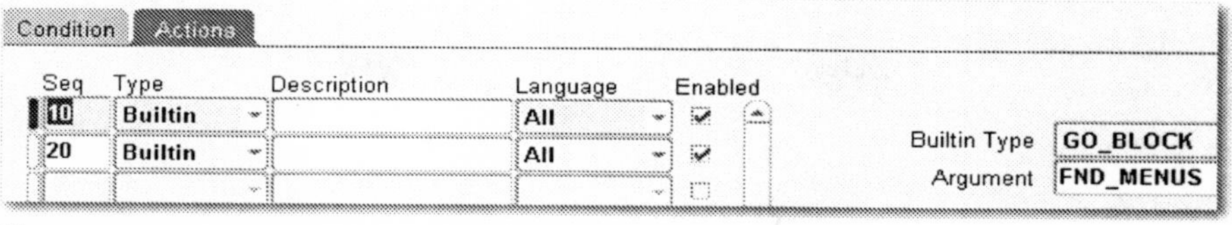

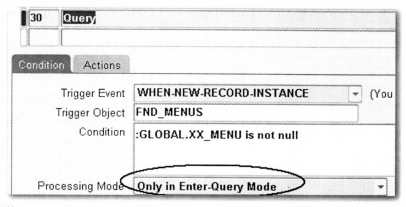

Illustration 7.20: Go to the correct block.
And:

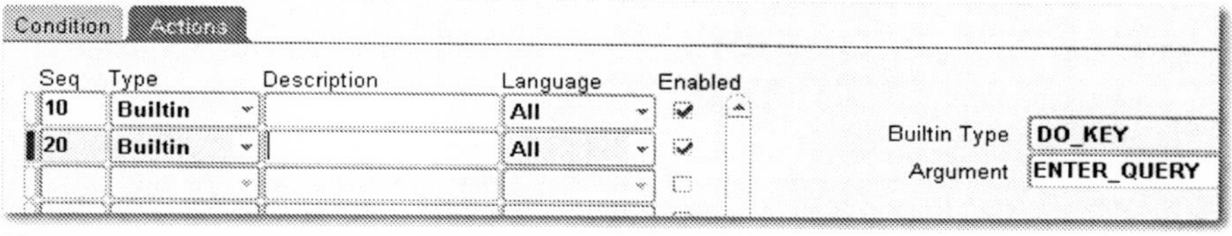

Illustration 7.21: Go in enter-query mode.

Step 8: Execute the query:

Illustration 7.22: Check if a query must be done.
And do the actual query in three steps:

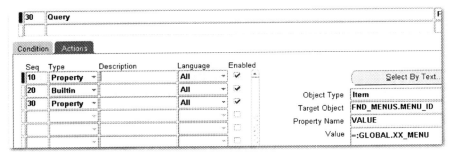

| | 30 | Query | | | | | F |

Condition | **Actions**

Seq	Type		Description	Language		Enabled	
10	Property	▾		All	▾	✓	▲
20	Builtin	▾		All	▾	✓	
30	Property	▾		All	▾	✓	
		▾			▾	☐	
		▾			▾	☐	
		▾			▾	☐	▾

Select By Text.

Object Type | Item
Target Object | FND_MENUS.MENU_ID
Property Name | VALUE
Value | =:GLOBAL.XX_MENU

Illustration 7.23: Fill in the query field.

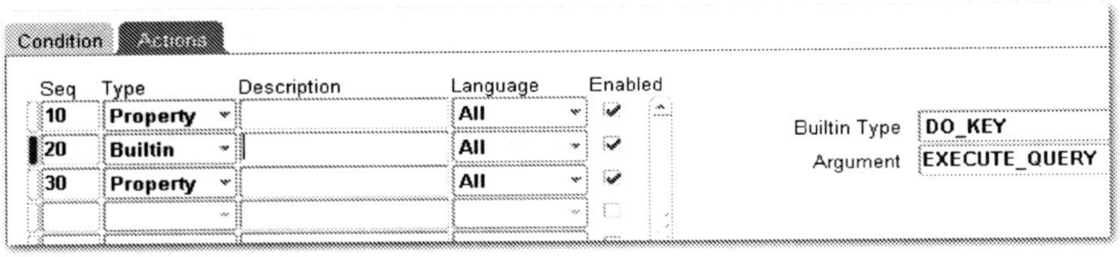

Condition | **Actions**

Seq	Type		Description	Language		Enabled	
10	Property	▾		All	▾	✓	▲
20	Builtin	▾		All	▾	✓	
30	Property	▾		All	▾	✓	
						☐	▾

Builtin Type | DO_KEY
Argument | EXECUTE_QUERY

Illustration 7.24: Do the query.

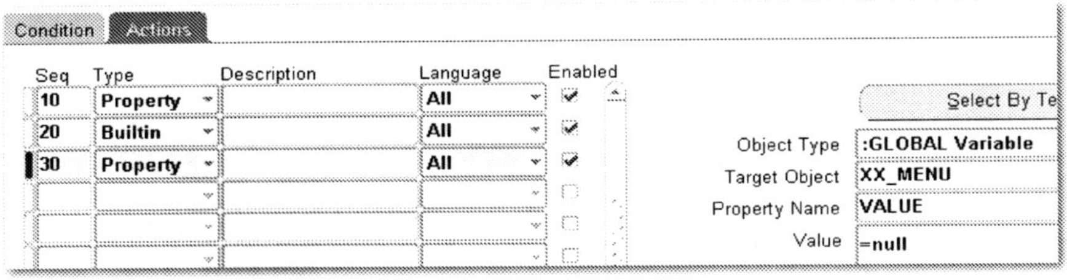

Condition | **Actions**

Seq	Type		Description	Language		Enabled	
10	Property	▾		All	▾	✓	▲
20	Builtin	▾		All	▾	✓	
30	Property	▾		All	▾	✓	
		▾			▾	☐	
		▾			▾	☐	▾

Select By Te

Object Type | :GLOBAL Variable
Target Object | XX_MENU
Property Name | VALUE
Value | =null

Illustration 7.25: Clear the Global variable.

108

Chapter 8

OA-Framework Personalization

OA-Framework pages can be personalized just as much as Forms based screens. You can make fields mandatory, give defaults, remove fields, adds Tips or change the order of columns. There are also other changes possible like inserting a button to easily export data to Excel or modifying the homepage layout. Try it out, it's easier than you think!

8.1.   What are Framework Personalizations?

Oracle Applications Framework (OA-Framework) has a layered architecture:

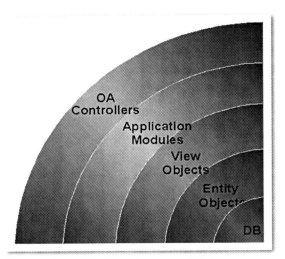

Illustration 8.1: The layers of OA-Framework.

Data comes from the database, and through these layers gets to the User Interface. In these layers data can be filtered (limited), ordered, validated, etc. You can use options to modify what can be seen and how you see it. You don't need to have a deep knowledge of these layers (unless you are a Java-developer interested in OA-Framework extensions), what really matters to you is the interface (the Framework interface) where personalizations can be made.

8.2.   Extensions and personalizations

OA-Framework pages can be changed in two ways: extensions and personalizations. For the first you need to build Java pages with Jdeveloper, that comply to the Framework standards (OA Extension metadata). Personalizations can be done through a web interface without Java knowledge.

8.3. Two Types of Personalizations

User Level Personalizations

This might suggest that a user is able to change the way a page looks. This is not the case. A *User Level personalization is a view (stored query)* that the user can use in a page. Like "Invoices from week 34", or "Invoices with amount > $1200.00". By selecting the view, directly the correct data will be displayed. Possibilities are:
- Order of Columns
- Column Prompts
- Hide or show Columns
- Query Filters

In other words, this is the OA-Framework counterpart of the Folder tools. This capability is not available in all search pages. It is possible if you have the "Save Search" button.

Administrative Level Personalizations

These are the real personalizations, making fields invisible, mandatory, giving defaults etcetera. This the OA-Framework counterpart of the Form Personalizations.

8.4. Characteristics of OA-Framework personalizations

- Patch-proof: Personalizations in Framework pages are actually stored in Database tables, and are therefore patch-proof.
- Not always directly shown: probably because of caching problems. Opening a new Browser to view the result might help.
- Possible corruption issues: In most fields the system does not verify the data that is entered. Therefore you should be careful as pages can become corrupt.

8.5. Administrative Level Personalizations

Personalization Context

The Personalization Context indicates in which context you are going to search for personalizations.

Choose Personalization Context
Choose the personalization context below by selecting a personalization value for each level.

Scope	Region: Request Simple Search Region
Function	[ ] Set to My Function
Location	[ ] Set to My Location
Site	☑ Include
Organization	Vision Communications (USA) [ ] Set to My Organization
Responsibility	System Administration [ ] Set to My Responsibility

Illustration 8.2: Context: for what context are the personalizations displayed?

After having given the context, you can set the personalization on that level. This works similarly to Profiles: you first search for a context (Site, Responsibility = Application Developer, User = Operations), then you can change the profile on the indicated levels to new values (this is called here: Personalization Levels):

.

Personalization Properties

Clear Personalization			Go	Choose Levels Displayed
	Original Definition Site		Organization: Vision Communications (USA) Responsibility: System Ad
Access Key Default	Inherit	Inherit	Inherit
Add Blank Value true	Inherit	Inherit	Inherit

Illustration 8.3: Values on different Personalization Levels.

114

Personalizations levels

Personalizations can be done on the following levels: Function, Industry, Localization, Site, Organization, Responsibility, Admin-Seeded User, Portal and User.

Personalization Level	Purpose
Function	Most precise level. Similar to Functions in Menus. A region can be modified to display a field if the Region is called in Function A. Otherwise the region is not modified.
Industry	For a specific vertical (Healthcare or Utilities)
Localization	For country specific modifications. Territory can be set through Preferences (or SSWA Preferences responsibility), or the profile ICX: Territory.
Site	Global personalizations, visible for everyone.
Organization	Useful in a multi-Org environment. For some organizations (Business Unit, Legal Entity etc) certain fields must be visible.
Responsibility	A customization visible for a responsibility.
Seeded User	Here you can create "Admin-seeded" end user views. The user can choose to work with this new view (layout) or not.
Portal-level	For customizations of eBS-regions in an Oracle Portal environment.
User	Personalization made by the user. A saved set of personalizations is known as a personalized "view" and can be selected and applied from the "View Personalizations" list.

If there are more personalizations for a page or region, all these are applied. First the Function level personalization, then the Industry personalization etc up to User level personalizations. Therefore the "lower" level personalizations will overrule.

Most logical for a larger organization are the Site level (for everyone) and the Responsibility level.

Profiles needed for Admin level Personalizations

Profile	Purpose
Personalize Self-service Defn	Set on User level, and this user sees the Personalize Page link. This is a System Profile.
FND: Personalization Region Link Enabled	Enables the Personalize Region link.
FND: Diagnostics	Enables "About this Page"
Disable Self-service Personal	If set on Site level, no personalizations will be shown. Good for support purposes (aka "Panic").

Tip: make a user with the 11.5.9 homepage

Personalizations may fail, since some data that you enter might not be validated. It is therefore possible that you make the homepage corrupt. Normally this would not be a problem, since you can switch off all the personalizations (with the profile "Disable Self-service Personal", described on page 116) . But if you cannot login, you cannot set this profile. Therefore you should make sure to have always a user to access the old 11.5.9 homepage. This can be done with the Profile "Self Service Personal Home Page". Give it the value "Personal Home Page" for the 11.5.9 Look-and-Feel or "Framework only" for the 11.5.10 Look-and-Feel. Once you have set this profile and logged in again, the homepage looks like this:

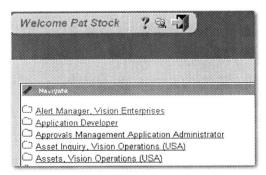

Illustration 8.4: The 11.5.9-homepage.

116

Setting the profiles for Admin level Personalizations

Before setting the personalization profiles the screen looks like this:

Illustration 8.5: Original Home-Page

After the profiles are set (and you have logged yourself in again!) the screen will look like this:

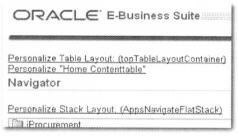

Illustration 8.6: Home page with personalization "on"

8.6. Guided exercises for User level Personalizations

Query Filters

Make a Query Filter that does only show the Expense Reports with Report Submitted date after 1 Feb 2000.

Step 1: Login as user Operations (or add to your user iExpenses).

Step 2: Go to tab page "Expense Reports". With the "Save Search" button, we can do a User level Personalization.

Step 3: Click on "Advances Search" and enter the search data:

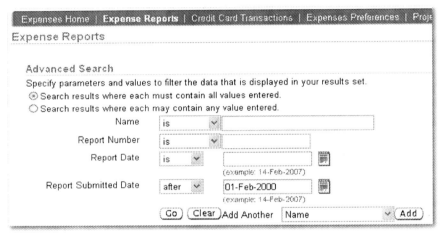

Illustration 8.7: iExpenses > Expense Reports > Advanced Search

Step 4: Click "Go":

Report Submitted Date	after	01-Feb-2000		

Report Number	Report Date	Report Submit Date	Report Status	Re
W14948	16-Jan-2003	05-Aug-2003	Paid	
W14944	09-Jan-2003	05-Aug-2003	Paid	

Illustration 8.8: The query result.

Step 5: Click "Save Search", give it a View name:

Illustration 8.9: Name of the saved view.

Step 6: Click "Apply and View". Again, click tab page "Expense Reports" and click "Views":

Illustration 8.10: The saved view. This is a User level Personalization.

As you can see, there is a "Personalize" button, we'll need in our next example.

Hide or show and rename Columns

Let's remove the "Receipts Status" column and rename "Report Status" to "Status".

Step 1: Click on the "Personalize" button, click on Update:

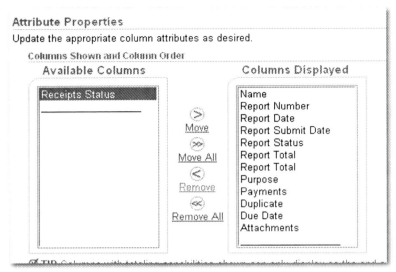

Illustration 8.11: Receipts Status has been hidden.

Step2: Click on "Renaming Columns / Totaling":

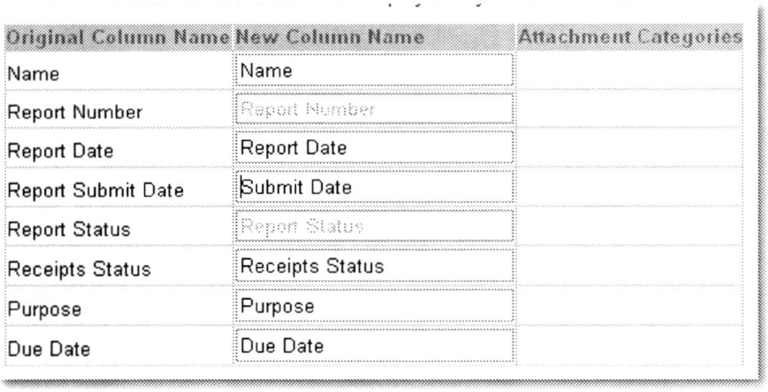

Original Column Name	New Column Name	Attachment Categories
Name	Name	
Report Number	Report Number	
Report Date	Report Date	
Report Submit Date	Submit Date	
Report Status	Report Status	
Receipts Status	Receipts Status	
Purpose	Purpose	
Due Date	Due Date	

Illustration 8.12: Mmm, the Report Status cannot be renamed, Let's rename Report Submit Date.

8.7. Guided exercises for Admin level Personalizations

Standard Branding

The "normal" Look-and-Feel is this:

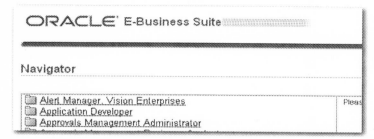

And the links look as follows:

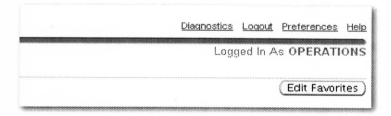

With System Profile **FND: Branding Size** set to Regular (= large) it will look like this:

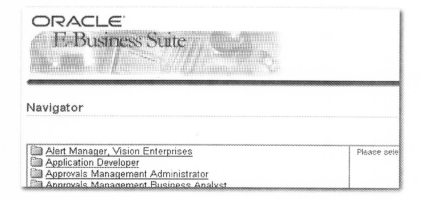

Also the buttons on the home page are large:

The Oracle images can be replaced with your own images (size: 134 * 23, format: gif) by placing an image on OA_MEDIA (on the application server) and setting the profile "**Corporate Branding Image for Oracle Applications**" to point to this image file.

Change the prompt of a Button

We are going to change the prompt of the Go button in Monitor Requests in System Administration responsibility.

Illustration 8.13: System
Administration > Monitor Requests

Step 1: Log on as the user for whom the Personalization Profiles are set.
Go to system Administration > Monitor Request:
Take a look at the screen. You will see lot of personalization links! Which one do you need?

Note 1: The personalization page link gives a list of all customizable objects. It can be difficult to find your object here.
Note 2: It is better to work with the Personalize Region link. Always try first the link just above the object that you want to modify.

Step 2: Click now on the following link:

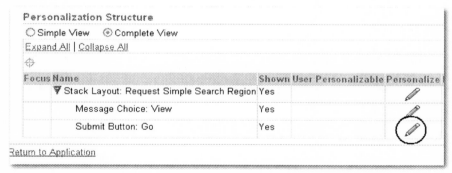

Illustration 8.14: System Administration > Monitor Requests (Personalization mode)

Step 3: The button will be displayed, and you will be able to personalize it with by clicking on the pencil icon to the right :

When you click on it lot of options will be displayed:

Most of them will be handled later.

Note 1: DO NOT PLAY with the CSS field. This may corrupt your Oracle environment, since invalid values are accepted by the screen.
Note 2: Rendered means: Displayed.
Note 3: This Region has apparently three levels: Site, Organization and Responsibility. And you see that (indeed) Site is overruled by Organization etc.

Step 4: Let's modify the value on Responsibility level, fill in: Go!
Step 5: Apply> Home > Logout. Login with your other username, go to Monitor Requests. The button looks good now:

Change a Label

Let's change Requests to Old Request.

Which link do we take? Well, there is no (Region) link above the object that we want to change, so we have to use the Personalize Page link (in the upper right corner of the screen).

Now we have a problem, since we have so many objects.

Note 1: since the object that we look for is in the upper region of the screen, it is probably also in the upper most region of the customizations page.

Note 2: search for Request: CTRL-F: Requests.

Step 1: Try this one:

Focus	Name	Shown	User Personalizable	Personalize
	▼ Page Layout: Requests	Yes		✎
⊕	▼ privacy			

Step 2: Change the title on site-level:

Step 3: Apply> Home > Logout. Login with your other username, go to Monitor Requests. The label looks good now:

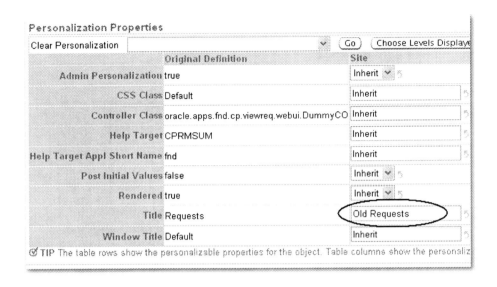

Remove a column from a table

Let's remove the Scheduled date from the table with the Requests date.

Step 1: Open again Monitor Requests.

Step 2: And again click on the link just above the object we want to modify:

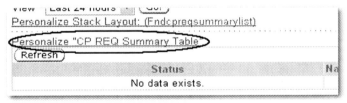

Again: a lot of changeable objects will appear. But, just search (CTRL-F) for "Scheduled":

Message Styled Text: Phase	Yes	
Message Styled Text: Scheduled Date	Yes	
Image: Details	Yes	

Step 3: Modify the object, and make it Rendered: false. Apply.
Result: it is gone.

Tip: Open an extra Oracle eBS session in which you are logged in as a "normal" user. After applying the modification, refresh the screen in the other session, the modification should be displayed.

Expand the number of rows returned in the table

Our table gives standard 15 rows per page. We want this to be expanded to 25 rows per page.

Step 1: Same modification link as in the previous exercise. Change the option: Records displayed.

Step 2: Apply and test:

Add a tip

We want to add a tip just above the Requests table, with the text: "Requests are the result of Concurrent Programs".
Step 1: Should we click the link above the table (with name = "CP Req Summary Table")? No, because this is the link of the table, and we want something above the table. So we click "Personalize Stack Layout". We can search for the tip, but it is not there. This is a new modification type: an addition. For this we have to use the "Create Item" button, and we are given three possibilities in this screen, but we are going to use the topmost:

s Name		Shown	User	Personalizable	Personalize	Reorder	Create Item
▽ Stack Layout: Request Summary L...		Yes			🖉	📇	🔁
	Separator: (Fndcpseparator)	Yes			🖉		
▽ Table: CP REQ Summary Ta...		Yes			🖉	📇	🔁
▽ Switcher: Status		Yes			🖉		
▷ case_name Fndcperroricon							

This one should be used, because with the second "Create Item" button, we would add an extra column in the Table.

Step 2: We make the Item Style: Tip, and give it an Id (some internal number – don't worry on this), and of course enter the Text:

Create Item
* Indicates required field

Level	Site ▼
Item Style	Tip ▼

Property	Value
* ID	323
Admin Personalization	true ▼
Attribute Set	
CSS Class	
Comments	
Extends	
Rendered	true ▼
Scope	.
Text	Requests are the result of Concurrent Programs
Tip Message Name	

Step 3: Apply and test. Looks weird, where is the Tip? It is below the Table:

✓	AP_INVOICE_PAYMENTS_ALL (Check
✓	AP_INVOICE_PAYMENTS_ALL (Check

(Refresh)
☑ TIP Requests are the result of Concurrent Programs

Step 4: We have to move it above the Table. Click on Reorder:

Name		Shown	User	Personalizable	Personalize	Reorder	Create Item
▽ Stack Layout: Request Summary L..		Yes			🖉	📇	🔁
	Separator: (Fndcpseparator)	Yes			🖉		

128

Place the Tip just below the separator:

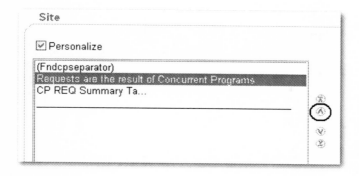

Step 5: Apply and test.

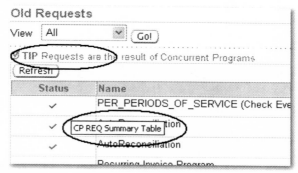

OK, the Tip looks good. But what a strange Tool Tip (CP REQ Summary Table).

Change a Tool tip

Note: Tool tips are meant as aid for visual disabled people. Be aware of this and avoid foolish or unnecessary changes.

The "Request Summary Table" is probably the easiest tool tip to practice on. Let's change it.
Step 1: Click "personalize CP REQ Summary Table". Personalize the Table:

Step 2: The Tool tip is the field named "Additional Text". Change the Tooltip to Request Summary Table:

Step 3: Apply and test.

Change the Branding Text

Changing the branding texts is only possible for some CRM applications and it works differently: within the Responsibility "CRM HTML Administration", you need to select Branding. We will not go into detail on this, since this is not applicable for all Framework pages.

Export Data to Excel

We want to insert an extra button, labeled "Excel", to export the requests.

Step 1: First we must find out the data source. In Oracle Applications Framework, data comes from View Objects (VO's). To find out the name of the VO, go to the Requests page and press "About this page" then click on the link "Expand All":

The column View Object displays repeatedly "RequestSummaryVO": This is what we need.

Name	Controller	Application Module	View Object	Vie
▽ pageLayout: View Requests	DummyCO	DummyAM		
▽ stackLayout				
▽ flowLayout: Request View Region	ViewRequestsPageCO	ViewRequestAM		
▽ stackLayout				
▷ stackLayout: (Fndcpreqsimplesearchreg)				
▷ header: Search	AdvancedSearchCO			
▽ stackLayout: (Fndcpreqsummarylist)				
separator: (Fndcpseparator)				
▷ tip: Requests are the result of Concurrent P...				
▽ table: Request Summary Table			RequestSummaryVO	
▽ switcher: Status			RequestSummaryVO Ss	
image: Error			RequestSummaryVO	
image: Warning			RequestSummaryVO	

Step 2: Now modify the page: home > Monitor Requests > Personalize Request Summary Table
Expand all fields and create an Item at the same level of the Refresh button:

▽ tableActions					
▽ Flow Layout: (ButtonContainerRN)	Yes			🖉	⧉
Submit Button: Refresh	Yes			🖉	

Item Style = Export Button, Additional Text = Export to Excel, Text = Excel, View Instance= RequestSummaryVO:

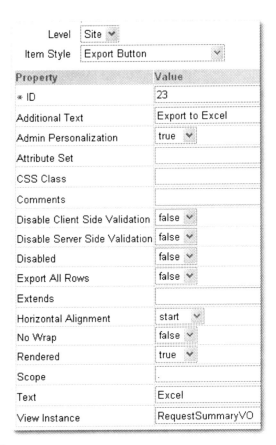

Step 3: Apply:

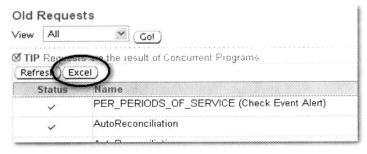

Step 4: and test:

A	B	C	D	E
Status	Name	Phase	Output	Request ID
	PER_PERIODS_OF_SERVICE (Check Event Alert)	Completed		4106186
	AutoReconciliation	Completed		4106095
	AutoReconciliation	Completed		4106084
	Recurring Invoice Program	Completed		4106082
	Recurring Invoice Program	Completed		4106081
	Recurring Invoice Program	Completed		4106080
	Final Payment Register	Completed		4106078
	AP_INVOICE_PAYMENTS_ALL (Check Event Alert)	Completed		4106051
	AP_INVOICE_PAYMENTS_ALL (Check Event Alert)	Completed		4106052
	AP_INVOICE_PAYMENTS_ALL (Check Event Alert)	Completed		4106053
	AP_INVOICE_PAYMENTS_ALL (Check Event Alert)	Completed		4106057
	AP_INVOICE_PAYMENTS_ALL (Check Event Alert)	Completed		4106055
	AP_INVOICE_PAYMENTS_ALL (Check Event Alert)	Completed		4106054
	AP_INVOICE_PAYMENTS_ALL (Check Event Alert)	Completed		4106056

Change the table display order

The end-user can change the display order of the requests by clicking on the column headers. But what if the requests should be always ordered first by Name (ascending), then by Scheduled Date (descending)?

Step 1: You know the drill by now: personalize The Request Summary Table. Personalize the Table:

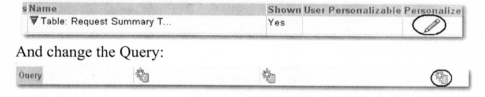

And change the Query:

Step 2: Apparently you cannot sort on something that isn't displayed, so lets order on Name and Phase:

As you can see, no data filtering is possible here. Some screens have this option, this one doesn't.

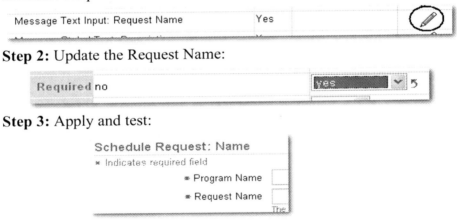

Step 3: Apply and test.

Make a field mandatory

Making a field mandatory is difficult to achieve in the Monitor Requests page, so, lets try with the Submit Requests page.
Step 1: Make the Request Name mandatory. Navigation path: home > Schedule Requests:

Message Text Input: Request Name   Yes

Step 2: Update the Request Name:

Required no   yes

Step 3: Apply and test:

Schedule Request: Name
* Indicates required field
     * Program Name
     * Request Name

Give a field a default value

Give the Request Name the default value Test.
Step 1: This is a property, with name: Initial Value. Unfortunately, in

134

Oracle 11.5.10R3 there is a bug: default do not show up. And important: the profile FND: OA:Enable Defaults needs to be set to Yes.

Step 2: If you work with a little older version, try to give the Request Name field in submit Request a default of "Test".

Step 3: Use the same customization link as for the Make Mandatory-exercise. Now with the following property: Initial Value = Test:

	Original Definition	Site
Access Key	Default	Inherit
CSS Class	Default	Inherit
Destination Function	Default	Inherit
Initial Value	Default	Test
Long Tip Region	Default	Inherit
Prompt	Request Name	Inherit
Read Only	false	Inherit ▼
Rendered	true	Inherit ▼
Required	no	yes
	false	Inherit ▼

Step 4: Apply and test:

✱ Program Name	
✱ Request Name	Test
	The name can later be

Make a link to another Form

Make a link between the Monitor Requests page and Submit Request.

Step 1: Create a button, just like the Excel Button as done on page 130,but with the following properties: Item Style: Button, Destination Function: FNDCPSRSSSWA, Prompt: New Request.

Step 2: Apply.

How do you determine the function name to be entered? Go to System Administrator > Application > Menu. Query the menu (System Administration), and click "View Tree":

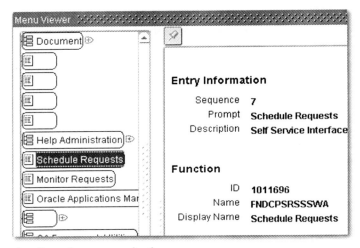

That's it, the function name is there.
Step 3: Test it:

8.8. Deploying Personalizations

Export to XML

Personalizations can be exported to an XML file with the responsibility "Functional Administrator". The profile "FND: Personalization Document Root Path" must be set at Site level, pointing to a directory on the mid-tier.
It should indicate what to export, and the destination path of the export.

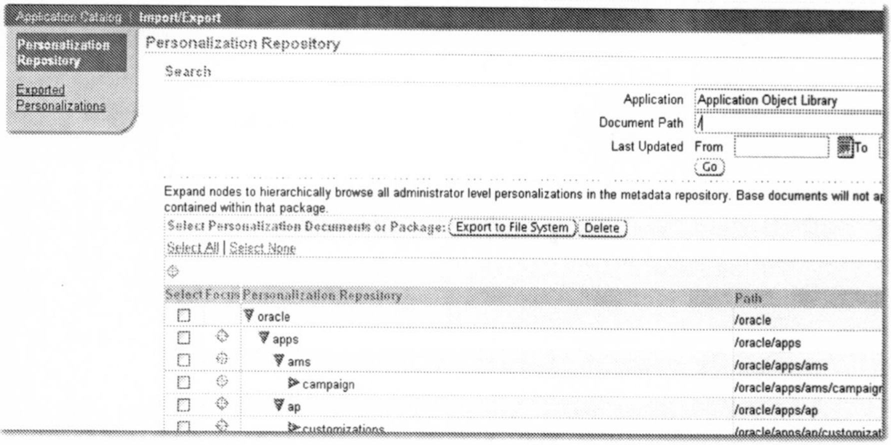

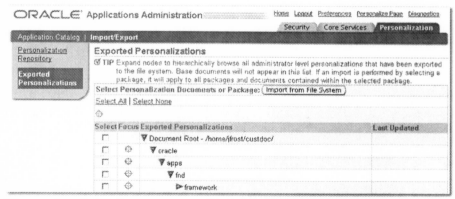

Illustration 8.15: Function Administrator > Personalization >
Import/Export.

Import from XML

Copy the XML file to the machine you want to import to, and go to the
import/export screen:

Illustration 8.16: Importing an XML file with Personalizations.

8.9. Exercises

Work with Workflow Administrator Web Applications > Developer Studio:
1. Make a field mandatory
2. Change the prompt of a field
3. Add a Tool tip
4. Remove a column from the search table
5. Change the order of the columns, and change a column header
6. Add an Export to Excel button to the table

8.10. Summary

In this chapter you have learned to work with OA-Framework Personalizations. We have covered customization profiles setting, customizations levels and compared in particular Admin level and User level administrations. This chapter also provided you with guided exercises on how to make fields mandatory, change result tables display order and add an Export-to-Excel button. At the end we have included some exercises on OA-Framework Personalizations.

Chapter 9

Flexfields

Personalization techniques for the Core-eBS Forms are powerful tools to implement changes to fields or prompt, but they do not allow you to collect and display any additional information. To do that you need Descriptive Flexfields. Descriptive Flexfields are fields that are built-in in some screens, via which you can store extra information in the database.

With Key Flexfields you can define the identifier structures in Oracle eBS. In other words, you can define how you categorize your financial data, and effect in this way your data reporting.

9.1. What are Flexfields?

Flexfields are fields that represent 1 field on the Form, but can expand to multiple subfields (called "Segments")[3]:

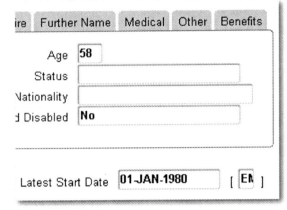

Illustration 9.1: Human Resources, Vision Enterprises > People > Enter and Maintain: a flexfield.

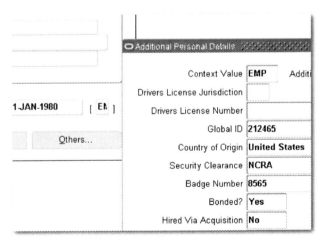

Illustration 9.2: The Flexfield expanded: lots of segments in one flexfield.

---

3   Way more information can be found in the Flexfields-book in this series.

Why are they called Flexfields?

Almost everything is flexible on a Flexfield:
- the number of segments (but limited by the database)
- the prompts of the segments
- the type of data you store in the segments
- the sequence of the segments
- extra security rules on the segments

9.2. Key and Descriptive Flexfields

There are two types of Flexfields: key flexfields and descriptive flexfields. A key flexfield appears on your form as a normal text field with an appropriate prompt. A descriptive flexfield appears on your form as a two character wide text field with square brackets [ ] as its prompt.

What are they used for?

Descriptive Flexfields are used for extra information which cannot be entered through the standard screens, for instance: you may want to keep record of the hobbies of your employees. Since this cannot be entered in the People screen in HR, you can use a Descriptive Flexfield for it.

Key Flexfields are used for data that is needed by Oracle E-Business Suite. For example, consider the codes your organization uses to identify general ledger accounts. Oracle E-Business Suite represent these codes using a particular key flexfield called the Accounting Flexfield. One organization might choose to customize the Accounting Flexfield to include five segments: company, division, department, account, and project. Another organization, however, might structure their general ledger account segments differently, perhaps using twelve segments instead of five.

Descriptive Flexfields

A descriptive flexfield appears on a form as an unnamed single character field between brackets. Just like in a key flexfield, a pop-up window appears when you move your cursor into a customized descriptive flexfield.

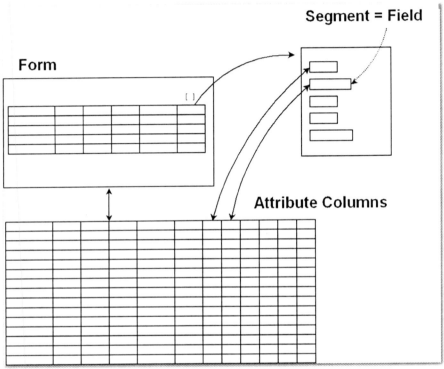

Illustration 9.3: The data of the DFF is stored in the same table as the data from the main form, but in the Attribute columns

A descriptive flexfield has the following characteristics:
- is not used by Oracle E-Business Suite
- contains data for the user
- does not interfere with eBS
- data is stored in the same table as the other data of the screen
  - in the Attribute columns
- there are hundreds DFF's

Key Flexfields

Most organizations use "codes" made up of meaningful segments (intelligent keys) to identify general ledger accounts, part numbers, and other business entities.

A key flexfield has the following characteristics:

- is used by Oracle E-Business Suite
- contains data for the user and Oracle eBS
- eBS relies on KFFs to work properly
- data is stored in a different table than the other data of the screen
  - o in the Segment columns
  - o in a code- combination table
- there are around 20 KFF's

Value sets

The fields (also called segments) of a flexfield must have a value set. A value set indicates what kind of data can be entered in the field. There are several types of value sets:

- Type none: validates nothing
  - o subtypes: char, number, date
- Type independent: fixed list
- Type dependent: fixed list, based on independent
- Type table validate: SQL query

Alias

Aliases are templates, used to facilitate entering the data of a Key Flexfield.

Cross validation rules

Cross validation rules are rules about several fields of a Key Flexfield. They are used for validating the data in the KFF.

9.3. Planning a Flexfield

The planning phase can be split into smaller, though still interrelated,steps:
- Decide which Flexfield to implement
- Learn about a specific flexfield
- Plan the structure
- Plan the segments
- Plan the segment validation
- Plan to use additional features
- Document your plan

Warning

It is recommended that you plan your Flexfields as thorough as possible, including your potential segment values, before you even starting to define them using Oracle E-Business Suite forms.
Once you have starting using your Flexfields to acquire data, you cannot change them easily.
Changing a flexfield when you have already stored data for it, may require a complex conversion process.

9.4. Guided exercises

View the structure of a Key Flexfield

The structure of a flexfield is the definition of the fields on the FF.
Let's find the structure of the General Ledger Accounting Flexfield.
Step 1: Go to System Administrator > Application > Flexfield > Key > Segments:

Step 2: Search for the Accounting Flexfield:

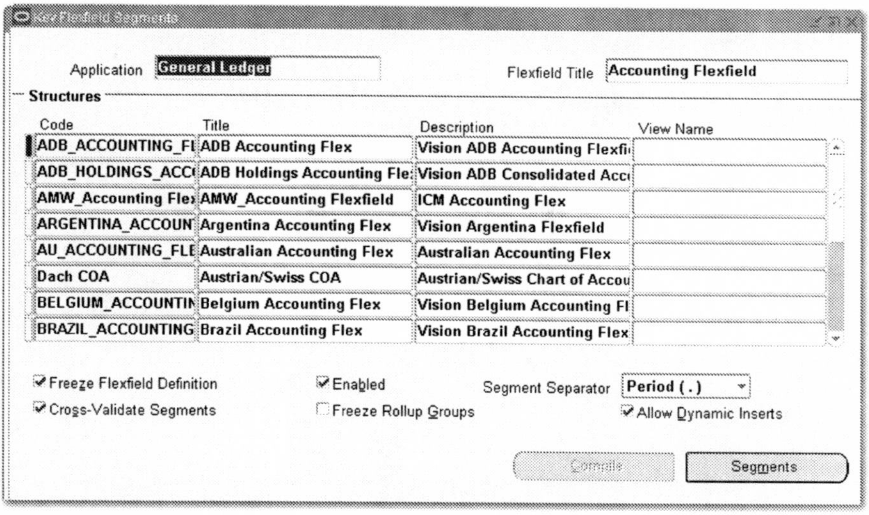

Wow, there are a lot of structures! Let's take a look in the "Argentina Accounting Flex" structure:

Step 3: select the Argentina structure and click on: "Segments":

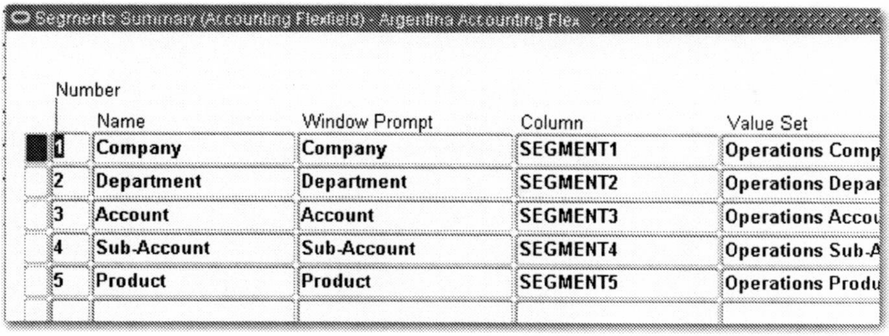

Illustration 9.4: The fields in the structure

Now you can see the fields.

Find the name of a Descriptive Flexfield

What is the name of the Descriptive Flexfield in the currencies screen in GL?

Step 1: Navigate to the screen: General ledger, Vision Operations (USA) > Setup > Currencies > Define:

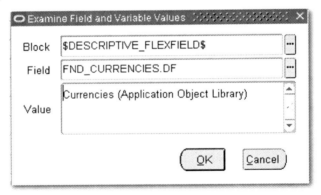

Step 2: Go to Help > Diagnostics > Examine, and give the Apps-password (standard it is apps).

Step 3: Go to block $DESCRIPTIVE_FLEXFIELD$, and the DFF(s) are shown:

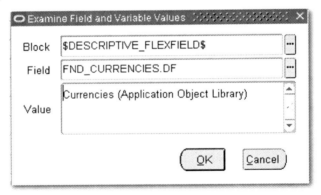

View the structure of a Descriptive Flexfield

Same as the structure of the Key Flexfield, but the navigation path is now: System Administrator > Application > Flexfield > Descriptive > Segments.

9.5. Exercises

1. Can you name the table that stores the Accounting Flexfield data? Hint: use responsibility "Application Developer".
2. Make a DFF in General Ledger, Vision Operations (USA) > Setup > Accounts > Summary with the field "Project?", with just two choices Yes or No. Hint: use an existing Value Set.

9.6. Summary

We had a closer look at flexfields, and explained where Flexfields data is stored, and what can be done with it. The chapter also provided more information on the location of DFF, and some exercises.

Chapter 10

Folders

In an Oracle E-Business Suite environment, there can be so much data, that finding you invoices or other financial information can be quite difficult. To facilitate retrieving of information, Oracle created Folders. Folders allows you to change the Layout (columns display and order) and the Query of certain core-eBS screens.

With Folders, you can make the work of your colleagues much easier.

10.1. What are Folders?

Folder forms are view-only forms supplied with the core applications. They allow users to change the layout and content of forms without customizing the forms.

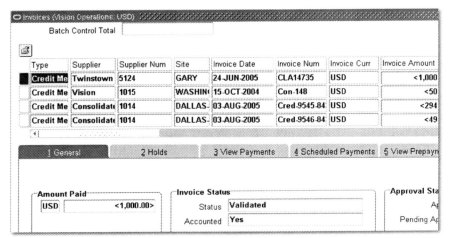

Illustration 10.1: Payables, Vision Operations (USA) > Invoices > Inquiry > Invoices

In a Form with Folder, the Folder option can be recognized by the enabled Folder symbol:

Overview of different personalization methods

In this handbook you have encountered several personalization methods. The table below describes the differences between the various personalization methods:

Personalization Method	Characteristics
Forms Personalization	<ul><li>introduced in 11.5.10.</li><li>works in all Core-eBS screens</li><li>change properties of existing fields / tabs</li></ul>
OA-Framework Personalization: Admin-level	<ul><li>works in all Framework-pages</li><li>change properties of existing fields / regions</li></ul>
OA-Framework Personalization: User-level	<ul><li>works in some Framework-pages</li><li>change layout and query</li></ul>
Flexfields	<ul><li>works in some Core-eBS screens</li><li>add columns for extra data</li></ul>
Folders	<ul><li>works in some Core-eBS screens</li><li>change layout and query</li></ul>

Working with Folders

Working with Folders is easy: click the Folder icon, and select the desired Folder:

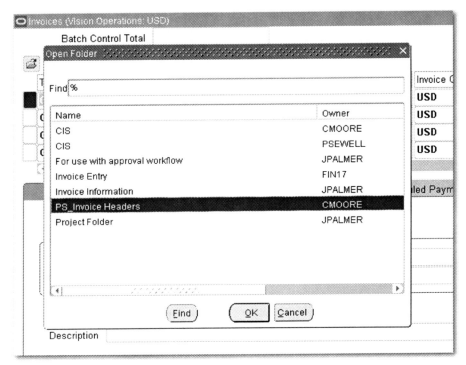

Illustration 10.2: Select a Folder

Click OK (query may take a long time), and see the new Layout and Data:

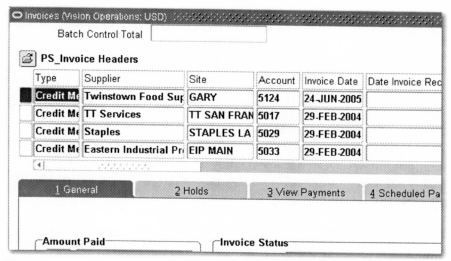

Illustration 10.3: The PS_Invoice Headers Folder is now used, notice the changed layout

10.2.   Making or Changing a Folder

Changing the appearance of a folder

You create or update versions of a folder by changing the following options as appropriate :
- Displayed fields
- Size of fields
- Order in which fields are displayed

This can be done from the Folder menu or by using the Folder tools. When you are satisfied with the appearance of the folder, save the definition.

Defining a folder query

 A folder query can be updated by entering and running the new required query and saving the folder afterwards. To view the new query go to Folder > View Query. The query can be reset to the default by selecting Folder > Reset Query.

For more complex queries it is possible to use a Clever Query as follows:
- Put the folder in query mode
- Enter :a in any displayed field
- Run the query

This will display a query/where window. Enter the Where Clause you want to execute in the window. You can reference any field associated with the folder, not just those displayed. To check available fields use Help -> Tools -> Examine then Block = FOLDER and Field = Use pick list to display available fields

You could write a query to select a range of values and use multiple fields.
Example; where Supplier Number between 100 and 300 and Invoice Date > 1-Jan-2006.
Run the query and save the folder.

10.3. Guided exercises

Make a Folder with different columns

Step 1: Start with the situation given in Illustration 10.3, select column "Date Invoice Received" and click Folder > Hide Field:

Step 2: After clicking on it, the column disappears:

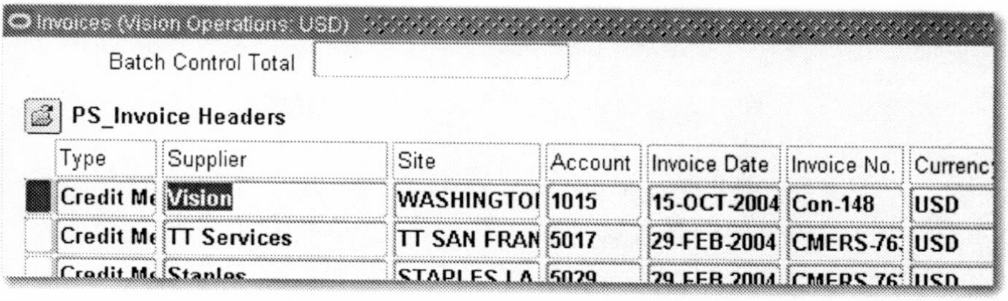

Type	Supplier	Site	Account	Invoice Date	Invoice No.	Currenc
Credit Me	Vision	WASHINGTOI	1015	15-OCT-2004	Con-148	USD
Credit Me	TT Services	TT SAN FRAN	5017	29-FEB-2004	CMERS-76:	USD
Credit Me	Staples	STAPLES LA	5029	29-FEB-2004	CMERS-76:	USD

Invoices (Vision Operations: USD)
Batch Control Total
PS_Invoice Headers

Illustration 10.4: Column "Date Invoice Received" is no longer displayed after selecting Hide Field

Step 3: Drag some Columns, and change a Column Prompt:

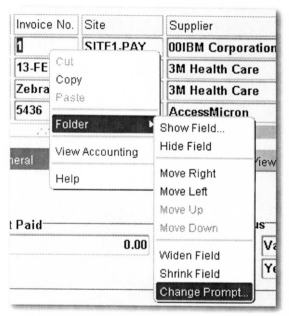

Illustration 10.5: Change a column prompt

Illustration 10.6: The changed column prompt

Change the query

Show only invoices with Invoice Date before 2005.
Step 1: First formulate a query by pressing F11:

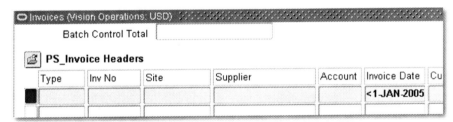

Illustration 10.7: Formulate Folder Query

Step 2: Click CTRL-F11

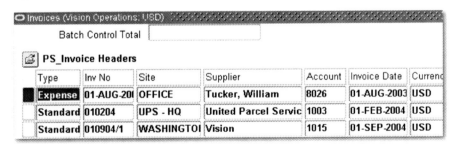

Illustration 10.8: Invoices with Invoice Date before 1-Jan-2005

Step 3: Save the Folder. Folder > Save As..

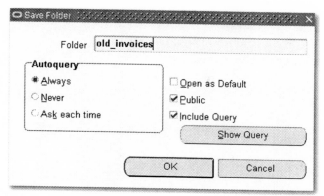

Illustration 10.9: Folder Options

And now you see the Folder Name in the screen:

10.4. *Folder Administration*

In the System Administrator responsibility, there is a screen which allows you to administer Folders: Application > Administer Folders. In this screen you can link a Default Folder to a Responsibility or a User. Folders are linked via a Folder Set to a Responsibility, and a Folder Set has always the name of the base table of the screen that you are modifying.

Folder Characteristics

Open the screen and search for your Folder:

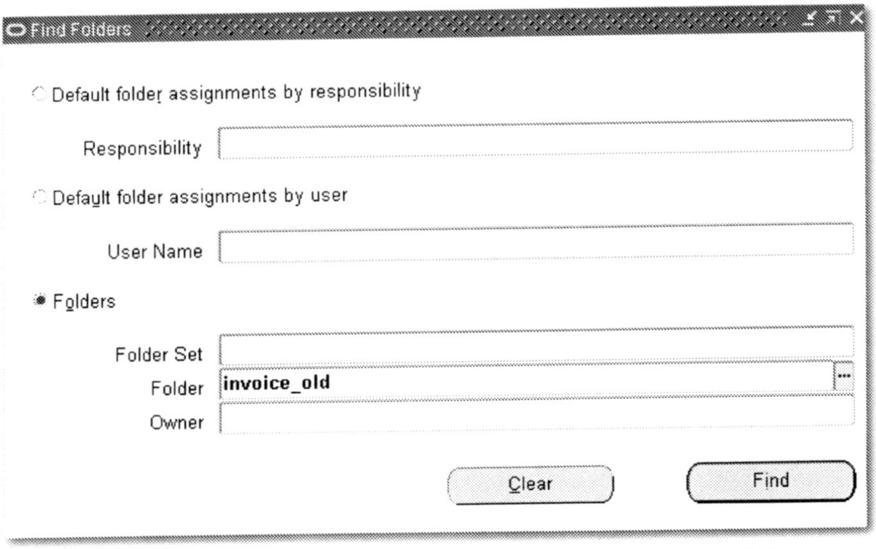

Illustration 10.10: System Administrator > Application > Administer Folders

Click on "Find", and select the checkbox "Public":

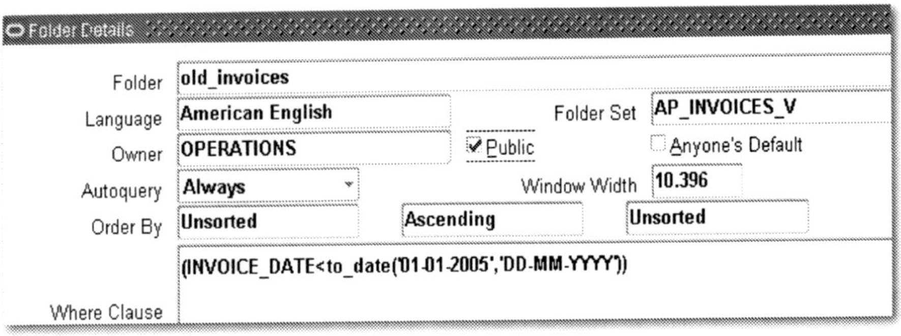

Illustration 10.11: Details of the Folder "old_invoices"

Link to a Responsibility

If you want to link a Folder to the Responsibility "Payables Archive Purge Vision Sweden" (so that users with this responsibility open this Folder by default), search a Responsibility:

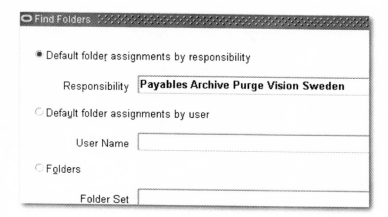

And link the Folder to this Responsibility:

Illustration 10.12: The Folder is linked to the Responsibility

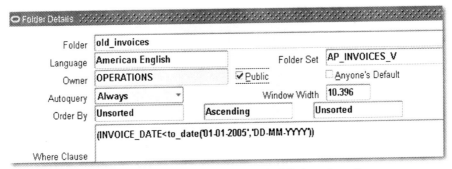

Illustration 10.13: Details of the Folder "old_invoices"

Link to a User

Linking to users works just as linking to a Responsibility, but it not recommended due to maintenance issues.

10.5. Exercises

Work with General Ledger, Vision Operations (USA) > Journals > Enter:

1. Change a prompt of a column
2. Hide a column
3. Add a column and reorder some columns
4. Save the folder under your name
5. Add a query to the folder; the screen should always opens with this query
6. Link your Folder to a Responsibility

10.6. Summary

In this chapter we have looked at the possibilities offered by Folders, both at layout and query level. We have also seen how a Folder definition can be linked to a Responsibility or User.

Chapter 11

Workflow Overview

Each organization works according to standard or customized processes. There are processes for creating Purchase Orders, for checking and approving incoming products, for Marketing Approvals, for vacation approvals etcetera. Oracle has automated these processes, and combined them with a monitoring tool and email alerts. This is called Oracle Workflow. It automates and streamlines the information flow through your organization.

11.1. What is a workflow?

A workflow is a flow of actions (steps) that must be executed one after the other to complete a certain task. For instance, an expense claim workflow would include (at least) the following actions:

- entering the expenses (or: querying the expenses from the database)
- sending the claim to the manager of the requestor
- approve or reject by the manager
  - o in case of a rejection: a message to the requestor that the claim was rejected, and why
  - o in case of an approval: a message to the payables department about the amount that must be paid

Oracle E-Business Suite has a Workflow Engine to process all this. Workflow is described in detail in an other book in this Series[4], and help can be found in the Workflow Forum[5].

11.2. Guided exercises

Create a Workflow in the Process Tab

Define a new Item Type that will be used as a workflow to create new users. This workflow will be added to the Process Tab in the Navigator for responsibility 'System Administrator' that normally has no Processes Tab.

Step 1: First launch the workflow builder on your Windows PC.
Start: *Programs -> Orahome -> Application developer -> Oracle Workflow Builder*

Note 1: the WF Builder must have the same version as the workflow server in the database.
Note 2: connection to the database is done via tnsnames.ora on your client

---

4   Oracle Workflow in the E-Business Suite
5   http://forums.oracle.com/forums/forum.jspa?forumID=72

Step 2: Create a new Item Type xx_PROC and a new runnable Process XX_NEW_USER via the Quickstart Wizard in the Workflow Builder.

- Internal name Item Type is xx_PROC and display name is xx Process Tab.
- Internal name Process is xx_NEW_USER and display name is xx Define New User.

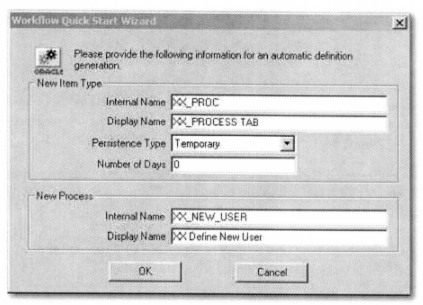

Illustration 11.1: File > Quick Start Wizard

Step 3: Define <u>two</u> new attributes. One called 'User Name' and one called 'Open Form'.

- Attribute 'User Name' has Internal name 'USER_NAME' and is of type 'Text'.
- Attribute 'Open Form' has Internal name 'FORM' and is of type 'Form'.

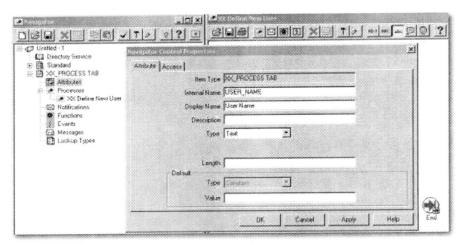

Illustration 11.2: Right click on 'Attributes' under the name of your new item type XX Process Tab and select 'New Attribute'

Step 4: Define a New Message 'User Message' with internal name 'USER_MESS' and put in the Body the help text you want to show to the user.

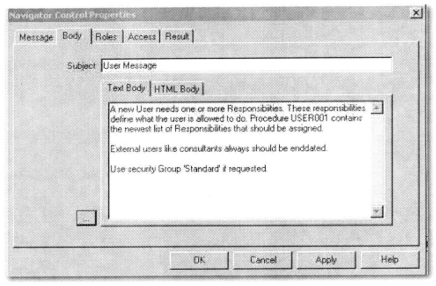

Illustration 11.3: The Message Body with fixed text

Step 5: Drag the 'Open Form' Attribute to the message 'User Message' in the Object Navigator. *Right-click to open the properties from the created local Attribute.*

- Switch the Source to 'Respond' (it takes input from the user).
- Point to the internal name of the 'Define User' form (FND_FNDSCAUS) as constant value.

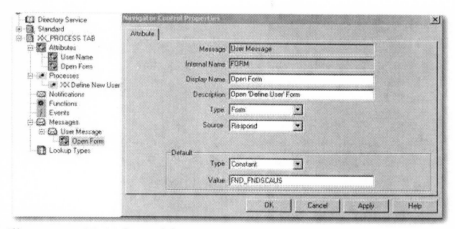

Illustration 11.4: One of the two Message Attributes

Step 6: Create a Notification 'New User Notification' with internal name NEW_USER_NTF as a shell for the created Message (again by right-clicking on Notifications and then selecting 'New Notification').

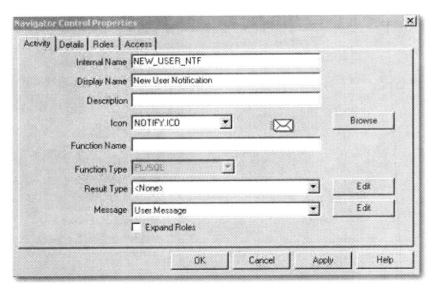

Illustration 11.5: The Notification with the Message linked to it

Step 7: Drag the Notification to the Process Flow on the right and create Transitions (arrows) with the help of the Right Mouse button.

- Create a transition from Start to Notification.
- Create a transition from Notification to End.

Step 8: The system needs the receiver information for Notification.

- Double click on the Notification in the process flow and enter the 'Item Attribute' (i.e. variable) 'User Name' as the 'Performer' (receiver) of the Notification in *T: Node*.

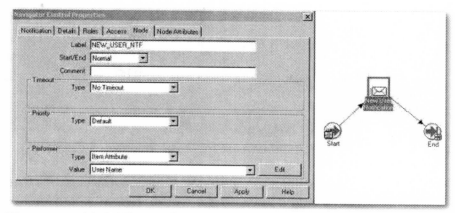

Illustration 11.6: The Performer is the receiver of the Message

Step 9: Save the Workflow in the database: File -> Save as (choose radio button Database).
- User and Password in the Vision Demo environment are 'apps'
- Connect to the SID of the environment you are working in (ask your DBA)

Click OK (saving will take some time)

Note: you can also save the .wft file locally.

Now we will continue to work within the System Administrator responsibility where we have to create a function pointing to this Workflow process - and the we have to add it to a menu.

Step 10: Create a function XX_NEW_USER that will call the created workflow. This must be of type 'PROCESS' and should point to the workflow through its parameters.
- Function name is XX_NEW_USER.
- User Function Name is 'xx New Apps User'
- Type is 'PROCESS'
- Parameters is XX_PROC:XX_NEW_USER (this is '*Internal name Itemtype*':'*Internal name process*')
- Save.

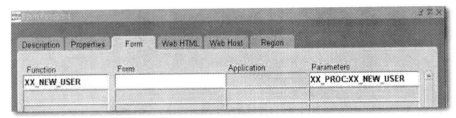

Illustration 11.7: System Administrator > Application > Function

Step 11: Create a (Sub)menu to attach the Function to a certain Menu (and responsibility). Add it to the Menu for the System Administrator FND_NAVIGATE4.0 (Navigator Menu - System Administrator GUI).
- Seq is 20x (x is your terminal number)
- Function is XX_NEW_USER.

Step 12 : Test the result in the System Administrator Menu
- Log in again to see the result.
- A process tab should be added to the menu including your Process.
- Your message should be Visible as explanation.
- Launch the flow by selecting the appropriate button
- Open the Form by clicking on the button "Open" or by double-clicking.
- Create a user and complete the step. If the step is not completed a notification will be sent to you (the user). In a more complicated workflow this could be someone else. If there were more steps involved it would notify the next person about the next step after completion.

11.5.9 Homepage to include Notifications

The Personal Homepage (PHP) gives access to the Menu (including Self-service), Notifications, Intelligence Information and Favorite Functions. When the Preferences responsibility is assigned to a user the PHP can be customized.

Functions can be accessed through the so-called 'Plugs' that are predefined by development.

170

- Change your Personal Homepage to include a tab with preferred functions and favorites.
- Switch to the PHP window through the Windows task bar (or via <Alt>-<Tab>).
- Select the icon 'Create and Modify Pages'
- Add a new page (Tab) via *B: New*
- Assign this page a name ('My Homepage') and save it by clicking on *Apply*.
- Click on *Edit* to split the new Homepage in two Columns (use the arrows for this).
  - Place your favorite Applications/URL's (plug 'Favorites') in the left column together with the Menu (plug 'Navigate').
  - Place the access to the Notifications in the right column (plug 'Worklist').
  - Click *Done* to save.
- Via the Hyperlink 'Customize' in the PHP you can set your preferences for a certain plug. You can set the preferences for Notifications to be sorted by Sent Date or to Show all Notifications Types sent in the last 10 days.
- If you have extra time, try to add specific favorites to your PHP, like the function 'Change Session Language' from the Preferences Responsibility. Via 'Custom' you can also add the link to http://metalink.oracle.com as a favorite.

11.5.10 Homepage to include Notification

You have to customize the homepage, and Render (=display) the Notifications Region. See Chapter 8 (starting on page 111) for more information on how to do this.

Using the Workflow Monitor

The Workflow Monitor is useful to diagnose problems that occur during processing. Search for Workflows reported errors in the last two weeks.
Step 1: Go to Workflow Administrator Web Applications.

Illustration 11.8: Workflow
Administrator Web Applications

Step 2: Search in the Status Monitor screen for the workflows with an error status:

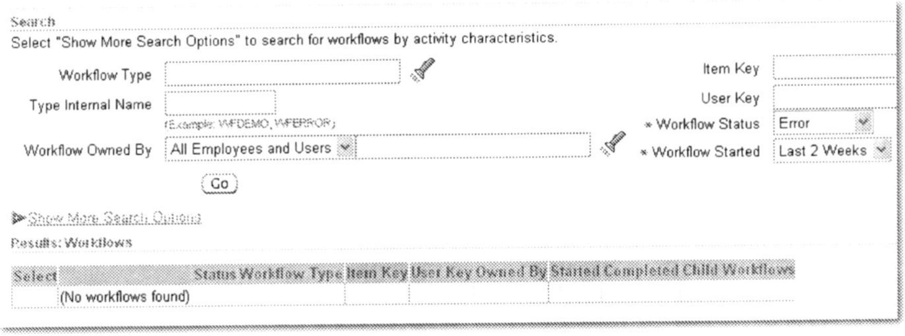

Illustration 11.9: No Workflows with an error status were found

In Vision 11.5.8 there are a lot of Email PO STUCK errors. A little investigation on Metalink[6] returns note 175325.1 which points to a faulty Workflow definition with too many END nodes.

---

6   http://metalink.oracle.com/

Using Status Diagram

Check the actual status of a running workflow.
Again, use the Status Monitor, now search for any status "In Process".
You will see some running Workflows:

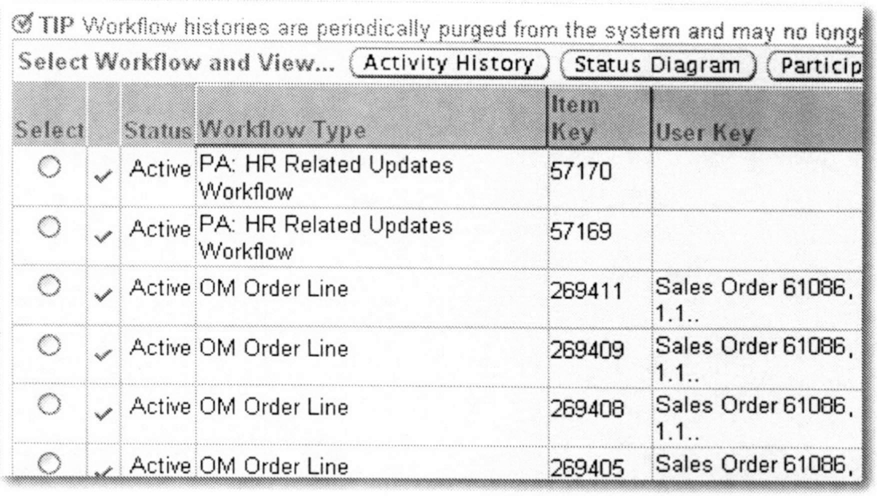

Select	Status	Workflow Type	Item Key	User Key
○	✓ Active	PA: HR Related Updates Workflow	57170	
○	✓ Active	PA: HR Related Updates Workflow	57169	
○	✓ Active	OM Order Line	269411	Sales Order 61086, 1.1..
○	✓ Active	OM Order Line	269409	Sales Order 61086, 1.1..
○	✓ Active	OM Order Line	269408	Sales Order 61086, 1.1..
○	✓ Active	OM Order Line	269405	Sales Order 61086,

Illustration 11.10: Workflows that are currently running in eBS

Select one and click "Status Diagram":

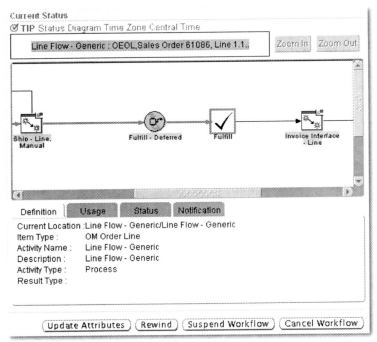

Illustration 11.11: The flow status, with Administrator's buttons

11.3. Exercises

1. If the Workflow Builder is installed on your PC's: create a Workflow in a process-tab, as described on page 164. Change *XX* with your initials.
2. Find two Workflows that are currently running.
3. Find a Workflow that has a status error. Can you see where did it get stuck?

Summary

In this chapter you have learned what can be done with Oracle Workflow, how Workflows can be monitored, and how to create a Workflow in the Process Tab. It ended with three exercises on this topic.

Chapter **12**

Oracle Applications Manager: Overview

An Oracle E-Business Suite system is technically very complex. It consists of a database (or more databases), one or more application servers, a Forms Sever, Reports Server, listeners, Advanced Queues, and more processes, instances and machines. Managing and monitoring all this has been always very difficult.

Luckily, Oracle has created the Oracle Applications Manager. Through this integrated web-based tool you can maintain and monitor most of the eBS-processes.

12.1. What is the Oracle Applications Manager?

Oracle Applications Manager (OAM) 11i is a system management console, built directly into the E-Business Suite. This tool is available for all 11i releases.

What OAM can be used for

You can use OAM 11i for a wide variety of system management tasks, including:

- Monitoring Components and Resources
- Diagnosing and Resolving Problems
- Managing Services
- Managing Concurrent Requests
- Managing System Configuration
- Managing Oracle Workflow
- Examining E-Business Suite Patch History
- Obtaining Patch Recommendations
- Understanding the potential impact of a patch

How to access it

Login as a User with Responsibility "System Administration":

Illustration 12.1: The Oracle Applications manager link in System Administration

After logging into OAM 11i, you will see the applications dashboard. Next to the Applications Dashboard you will see the site map tab:

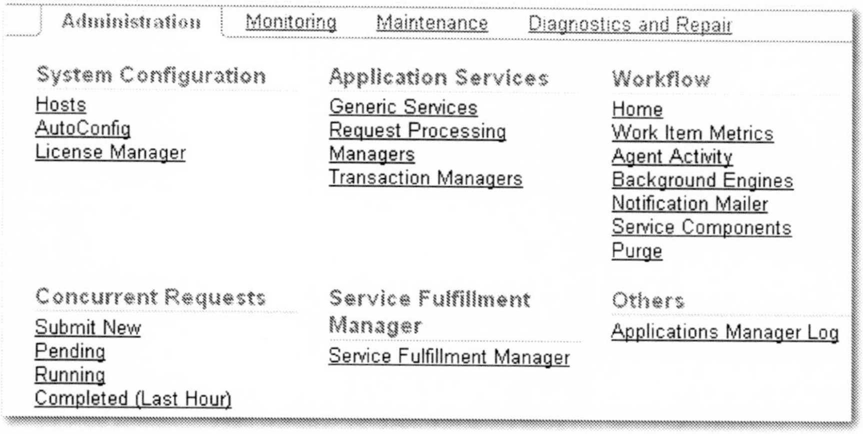

Illustration 12.2: Site map in OAM

Alongside these tabs, on the top right corner you will see the 'navigate to' drop-down list which gives you a 'shortcut' to the following areas:

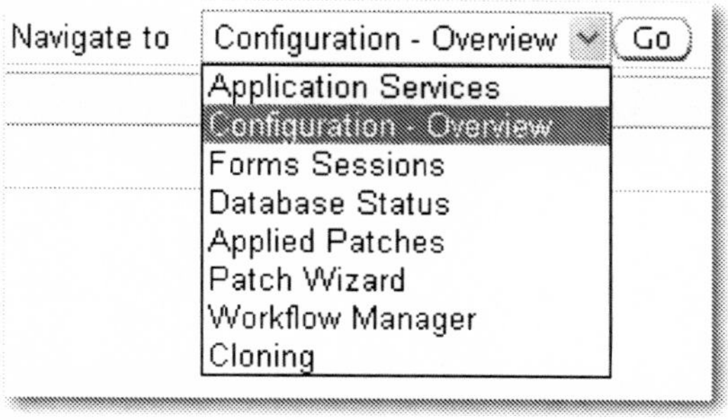

Illustration 12.3: Navigation shortcuts

Select one then click "Go". Way more information can be found on the Oracle Forum "Managing Oracle Applications"[7].

OAM Applications Dashboard Collection

The Concurrent Program "OAM Applications Dashboard Collection" must be scheduled to make sure the dashboard displays up-to-date information. This Concurrent Program can be accessed via System Administrator > Requests > Run.

---

7   http://forums.oracle.com/forums/forum.jspa?forumID=40

12.2. Guided exercises

Which profiles were changed last week?

Go to "Configuration – Overview" > Site Level Profiles:

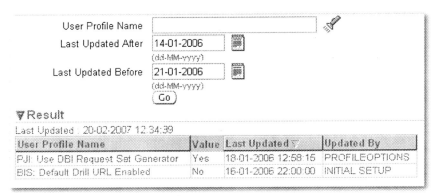

Illustration 12.4: Profiles changed last week

Which Operating Units are there in the system?

Go to "Configuration – Overview" > Application Information:

Organization ID ▽	Name
7047	Vision India Mumbai
7046	Vision India Hyderabad
6946	Vision Romania
6666	Progress UK Health Services
6646	Progress BE
5379	Vision Russia

Have Requests been submitted during the last hour?

Application Dashboard > Performance > Running Concurrent Requests > Simple Search:

Quick Searches:

Requests submitted in the last one hour
Pending Requests submitted in the last 24 hours
Errored Requests submitted in the last 24 hours
Completed Requests in the last 24 hours that ran for more than 60 minutes

Illustration 12.5: Quick Search on the Requests

Details	Request ID	Program	Phase	Status	Requestor
Show	4106109	OAM Applications Dashboard Collection	Pending	Scheduled	SYSADMIN
Show	4106108	OAM Applications Dashboard Collection	Completed	Normal	SYSADMIN
Show	4106107	OAM Applications Dashboard Collection	Completed	Normal	SYSADMIN
Show	4106106	OAM Applications Dashboard Collection	Completed	Normal	SYSADMIN
Show	4106105	OAM Applications Dashboard Collection	Completed	Normal	SYSADMIN

Illustration 12.6: Requests submitted during the last hour. You can drill down for details

Are there known Security problems?

Application Dashboard > Security. Here you can run the Security Test Failures:

Focus	Test Name	Failure Time	Diagnose
	Failure Level		
	Error		
	FND		

How many Requests are running now:

Application Dashboard > Services Up > Activity Monitors:

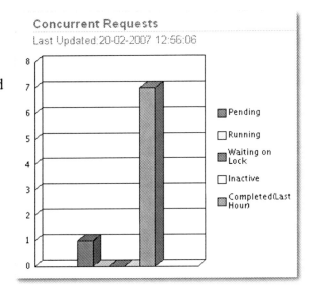

12.3. Exercises

1. What is the availability status of the Database?
2. Which products (modules) are you licensed to use?
3. Are there any messages stuck in Advanced Queues? These queues are called Workflow Agents.

12.4. Summary

In this chapter we have looked at some of the possibilities of the Oracle Applications Manager. The OAM allows you to monitor the status of the database, the queues, the listeners and the servers and it can also run some Security tests, purge processes, store and retrieve historical data about Requests.

Alphabetical Index